SELLING WITHOUT CONFRONTATION

Jack Greening

SOME ADVANCE REVIEWS

"An excellent sales tool for both the new and seasoned sales-person. Greening's many years of sales comes through with some great sales techniques. I've been in sales and marketing for 25 years and this book is certainly a tremendous sales aid for me."

Thomas D. Nelms
Manager, Sales Training
The Kelly-Springfield Tire Company

"Filled with real life sales situations. It offers a good over-view for a newcomer to the exciting world of sales. . . . The greatest value of this book is the emphasis Greening places on the importance of understanding the customer's point of view."

Victoria Anne Shire
General Manager, Marketing, Planning, and Advertising
Northern Illinois Gas Company

"The blueprint for a successful sales plan. . . . Concise and informative."

Bernard E. Wieland
Vice President, Sales & Marketing
Unarco Material Handling, a UNR Company

"An easy-to-read and insightful collection of proven tips and techniques. . . . A toolbox must for everyone from the cub to the most seasoned professional salesperson. . . . You will increase sales (and of course, profits and income) and reduce sales costs and frustrations by applying these principles."

John B. Nofsinger
Vice-President, Marketing and Administration
Material Handling Industry

"Greening takes us through the complete sales process from pre-call planning and preparation to post-call analysis and follow-up. The book's action plans and exercises make it a very usable, practical sales tool for sales people of all experience levels."

Don A. Sultzbach
Senior Vice President, Sales and Marketing
United National Bank & Trust Company

"A reliable resource for the sales trainee and the veteran alike. Like the old pros of any profession, Greening sticks with the basics; his philosophy of preparation, practice, and approaching any selling situation from the listener's vantage point are cornerstones of selling success."

Jack L. Florin
Director of Advertising & Promotion
The Kelly-Springfield Tire Company

"Jack's checklist approach makes sure that there will be no surprises during face-to-face interaction with the client. It answers . . . key questions for anyone who wants to influence someone else to buy."

Pete Schaeffer
Human Resource Development Manager
The Hoover Company

NOTES FOR PROFESSIONAL LIBRARIANS
AND LIBRARY USERS

This is an original book title published by The Haworth Press, Inc. Unless otherwise noted in specific chapters with attribution, materials in this book have not been previously published elsewhere in any format or language.

CONSERVATION AND PRESERVATION NOTES

The paper used in this publication meets the minimum requirements of American National Standard for Information Sciences–Permanence of Paper for Printed Material, ANSI Z39.48-1984.

Selling Without Confrontation

HAWORTH Marketing Resources
Innovations in Practice & Professional Services
William J. Winston, Senior Editor

New, Recent, and Forthcoming Titles:

Long Term Care Administration: The Management of Institutional and Non-Institutional Components of the Continuum of Care by Ben Abramovice

Cases and Select Readings in Health Care Marketing edited by Robert E. Sweeney, Robert L. Berl, and William J. Winston

Marketing Planning Guide by Robert E. Stevens, David L. Loudon, and William E. Warren

Marketing for Churches and Ministries by Robert E. Stevens and David L. Loudon

The Clinician's Guide to Managed Mental Health Care by Norman Winegar

Framework for Market-Based Hospital Pricing Decisions by Shahram Heshmat

Professional Services Marketing: Strategy and Tactics by F. G. Crane

A Guide to Preparing Cost-Effective Press Releases by Robert H. Loeffler

How to Create Interest-Evoking, Sales-Inducing, Non-Irritating Advertising by Walter Weir

Market Analysis: Assessing Your Business Opportunities by Robert E. Stevens, Philip K. Sherwood, and Paul Dunn

Marketing for Attorneys and Law Firms edited by William J. Winston

Selling Without Confrontation by Jack Greening

Persuasive Advertising for Entrepreneurs and Small Business Owners: How to Create More Effective Sales Messages by Jay P. Granat

Marketing Mental Health Services in a Managed Care Environment by Norman Winegar and John L. Bistline

Selling
Without Confrontation

Jack Greening

The Haworth Press
New York • London • Norwood (Australia)

© 1993 by Jack Greening. All rights reserved. No part of this work may be reproduced or utilized in any form or by any means, electronic or mechanical, including photocopying, microfilm and recording, or by any information storage and retrieval system, without permission in writing from the publisher. Printed in the United States of America.

The Haworth Press, Inc., 10 Alice Street, Binghamton, NY 13904-1580

Mammoth Enterprises and all the characters in this book are products of the author's imagination. Any resemblance to actual companies and persons, living or dead, is entirely coincidental.

Caricatures by Bob Stanley.

Library of Congress Cataloging-in-Publication Data

Greening, Jack.
    Selling without confrontation / Jack Greening.
      p.   cm.
    Includes bibliographical references and index.
    ISBN 1-56024-326-0 (acid free paper).
    1. Selling. I. Title
HF5438.25.G735   1993
658.8'5–dc20

92-21789
CIP

For salespeople . . . about salespeople . . .
by a salesperson . . . in salespeople's language.

Salesperson: An optimist who seeks out
ways to help the client benefit.

–Jack Greening

CONTENTS

ABOUT THE AUTHOR

Jack Greening is a leading international salesman with thirty-five years of sales and marketing experience. As a sales representative, field manager, national sales manager, and sales training manager, he has had extensive sales seasoning in North America, Europe, and the Middle East, with an outstanding record of sales achievement. He is the owner of Productive Communications, a consulting organization specializing in sales and marketing systems and methods. Greening has worked with many Fortune 500 executive officers developing effective in-house custom-designed programs, including General Motors, Standard Oil, Goodyear, Hoover, Blue Cross and Blue Shield, and The American Institute of Banking. A university lecturer, guest speaker, trainer, and business consultant, he lives in North Canton, Ohio.

This book is dedicated to those people who earn their living in the loneliest, and most demanding, frustrating, and exciting business there is . . . Professional Selling.

To the career salespeople who bring new products and services to buyers, who find new methods to use existing products and services, and who enrich our lives in the process.

To the people who work in a profession that requires guts, determination, tenacity, and a total commitment to the belief that they can be of help to others.

To the people who can go from the depths of despair to the heights of elation day after day, and still smile at the world.

I affectionately hope that this reference book will lift you up when you are eating alone in that empty dining room or in your hotel room.

Without you there would be no movement of goods and services. There would be no private sector. Free enterprise would cease to exist.

Observation

The practical, field-tested skills covered in this reference book have been developed for both the "newer" and the "veteran" salesperson. The newer salesperson will be able to use it as a foundation upon which to build his or her selling strategies. The veteran salesperson will be able to re-establish the fundamental skills that can slip away over a period of habit-forming activities.

Jack Greening
North Canton, Ohio

Preface

I have always wanted to write a book for salespeople. The urge was there. The discipline, dedication, and commitment was something else.

Oh, yes! I had visualized the accolades–the attention that comes to the successful author. I had fantasized receiving the adulation of beautiful women. Perhaps a trip to Trump Castle. Lined up behind the beautiful women were the chief executive officers patiently waiting their turn to offer me a lucrative consulting contract. There were the lecture tours–fabulous fees . . .

Coming back to earth, there still remained the lack of discipline, dedication, and commitment.

Many years ago when I studied journalism, my professor told me, "Greening, Robert Ludlum you are not. You have good, creative ideas, but you lack the discipline necessary to write effectively. I suggest that you first concentrate on a subject about which you have a modicum of knowledge and understanding and something to say."

I procrastinated for about thirty years.

Today, after many years as a service representative, salesman, field sales manager, trainer, university lecturer, guest speaker, and self-employed business consultant, I again have the urge. If you are reading this book, then I have also mastered the discipline necessary to do my homework.

Acknowledgements

One of the advantages enjoyed by those of us who work in human resource development is the opportunity to communicate with many people in a variety of professions, businesses, and industries. Therefore, I thank the many salespeople, sales managers, and, yes, buyers with whom I have worked and who have contributed in no small way to the material that follows.

Introduction

In today's world of accelerating change, professional salespeople must be counselors, problem solvers, innovators, and, above all, practitioners of effective two-way communication. The marketplace is changing rapidly. Competition is fierce and coming on strong. Clients are more demanding than ever before.

The objective of this book is to help salespeople meet the challenge of achieving success in this highly competitive marketplace and more effectively sell their products and services to increase sales and profits. The professional salesperson must look at his or her products and services as the client views them, *not* what it is and how it works, but rather what it will do for the client.

Each selling technique plays a role in moving the client's thought process from the initial contact to a successful commitment to the project.

The client will compare products and services with others available. He will expect to see advantages that the alternative source does not have to offer. If the services are of equal value, he will accept the one that is most effectively presented.

The client will search for weaknesses. He will expect to see testimonials and proof if there is any doubt in his mind.

The client will look for guidance in making a decision. A desire must be created–a need must be met–if the commitment is to be made.

In this book, we will share proven, practical skills that are necessary to think and act as the client thinks and acts. To be able to present the solution from the client's side of the table. I have called this approach *selling without confrontation.*

Chapter 1

Planning for a Productive Sales Call

Imagination: The act of taking up residence in someone else's point of view.

—Adapted from John Erskine

- I will ask myself: "Why am I making this call?"

- I will plan to have a purpose for my sales contact.

- My purpose is to help my client.

- I will research my client's situation to find areas of need that can be explored.

- I will not waste my client's valuable time by making play-it-by-ear calls.

There is a logical, sequential flow to the skills required in the seller/buyer negotiating process–from the planning and preparation stage to a successful conclusion, and on to post-call analysis and follow-up. The first step is planning.

PLANNING IS A DIFFICULT ACTIVITY FOR SALESPEOPLE

Planning is often considered an administrative task. It is a time-consuming, and tedious function for some salespeople. Good planning requires effort on the part of the salesperson, including the right attitude toward this important part of the sales strategy. Without good planning, many sales calls finish up as goodwill calls (at least this is what they are called) or wasted calls, and result in a loss of client acceptance and a potential erosion of hard-earned business relationships.

I remember a typical situation that happened many years ago when I sold soaps and detergents door-to-door. Our sales force was trained in the "Charge up San Juan Hill" school of selling. Each morning we attended a dawn meeting. We would stand on chairs lustily singing the company marching song, while the sales managers gleefully threw boxes of detergent at us. Because of their highly emotional state at the time–wild eyes, frothing at the mouth–the managers would usually miss their targets. Following this emotional conditioning, we would storm out of the building, leaping imaginary obstacles, ready to sell the world.

Invariably, we would come to a full stop on the street and the following dialogue would ensue:

"Where are you going?"

"I don't know. I may try Market Street today. How about you?"

"Well, I haven't hit the South Side lately; maybe there is some business over there."

Then, with all of our energy spent, we would repair to the coffee shop to discuss our problem.

A LOOK AT THAT DESPICABLE SUBJECT–PAPERWORK

Before we can fully appreciate the value of sales call planning, we need to take a look at this matter of paperwork.

For many salespeople, planning is paperwork–a natural enemy to be shunned at all costs.

I often open the planning module of a training workshop with a statement such as, "I really like paperwork." This is good for a few sidelong knowing glances, raised eyebrows, and a smile or two. I follow with: "Paperwork belongs in the bathroom." If I have a document such as a planning action checklist or a progress report, then I have selling tools that will help me do a better job:

1. Developing selling blueprints ahead of time will eliminate the barrier of cross viewpoints (selling blueprints will be addressed in Chapter 5):

   The client's viewpoint: "What will it do for me?"
   The seller's viewpoint: "What do I have to sell? How does it work?"

2. Written pre-call research will provide areas to explore on that first fact-finding call.

3. Pre-post call checklists will ensure that we have a track on which to run.

4. A follow-up sales call action plan can be based upon:

   - Re-establishing the client's objective.
   - Presenting the solution.
   - Setting up a market analysis.
   - Developing a proposal or bid.
   - Joint activities to achieve the objective.

   What are some of your sales call follow-up activities?

   _____

   _____

   _____

   _____

5. A progress report helps us to bridge from one sales contact to the next.

Because an order is usually the result of a series of sales contacts, most experienced salespeople that I know use worksheets to build their selling action plans for each client. These are not unnecessary papers that are required by a watchful management. They are documents that *work* for the salesperson. Look at planning as a necessary part of effective selling–which it is. Give this activity the importance that it deserves. If it helps, use it!

Recently, John Harris, a sales friend of mine, said, "Come to think of it, I always plan my vacation time very carefully, right down to the last detail. I plan my activities with my wife, my kids; yet I spend very little time planning my sales contacts." Consider the fact that all of John's personal activities could ultimately be affected (positively or negatively) by the amount of planning that he puts into his selling strategies.

LACK OF FORMAL TRAINING
IN THE SKILL OF PLANNING

Very few of us receive any formal training in the skill of effective planning. To varying degrees, we receive training in product or services knowledge, selling skills, company policies, time and territory management, handling objections, and, hopefully, closing techniques. We must develop sales call planning through trial and error. This includes our clients' participation and, as a result, we can lose our prestige and credibility. The client is thinking, "Why is this person here? What can he or she do for me?"

Remember the salesperson who said, "I make 22 calls a day. I could make 27, but every now and then someone asks me what I sell." New salespeople are often given a catalogue, price sheets, an order pad, and instructions from their manager to "Call me if you get into trouble."

PLANNING IS NOT A NATURAL
ATTRIBUTE FOR SALESPEOPLE

We migrate to the selling profession because we find it hard to work effectively in a structured, supervised work environment. We like to work within the framework of company policy but still be our own boss and be able to move freely. Couple this with a natural enthusiasm and a desire to work with people, then it is understandable that we are not detail-oriented people. This can create real problems. Have you ever:

1. Had a client say to you, "Why are you taking up my valuable time?"

2. Used the expression "I was in the area and thought I should stop by"?
3. During your presentation, watched the client become a "wide-awake sleeper"?
4. Had the client's secretary keep you occupied at the front desk as the buyer escaped out the back door?
5. Asked yourself, "Why am I making this call?" and been unable to answer your own question? Then, my friend, you have not planned the call.

"Plan my calls? I don't have time," old Paul ("Personality Plus") Perkins told me the other day. P.P. radiates enthusiasm, charisma, and confidence. He has an infectious personality. People around him get excited without understanding why. He doesn't walk anywhere, he breezes along–head purposefully thrust forward–eyes bright and alert. You recognize instinctively that P.P. believes that he knows where he is going (but not necessarily why) since his body tends to "point" as a good hunting dog points. He is always in the center of things–in the middle of the largest group–holding forth with his latest story. It is of no real import to him whether or not anyone is listening; he is his own best audience, and he genuinely appreciates listening to himself.

P.P. makes social calls! He never establishes a purpose for his sales calls. He happily jumps into his car each morning and drives off in whichever direction it happens to be facing. He is a friendly chap who talks about himself and, I suspect, to himself. P.P. does have some "enthusiastic non-users." l don't know how much longer he will be working for Mammoth Enterprises.

PLANNING IS THE KEY
TO PRODUCTIVE SALES CALLS

Planning will reduce the problems caused by hit-or-miss sales contacts that have no real purpose or direction. The value of planning sales contacts really got through to me some years ago when, as a field sales manager, I made a sales call with one of my salesmen on a major client. As soon as the buyer and I sat down alone in

P.P. Perkins "points" toward an unknown destination.

his office he started to jump all over me: "I don't want your salesman calling here again. He wanders around chatting to all of my office staff and distracting them from their work. He drinks coffee for an hour, and then has the nerve to ask me if everything is OK. He must have a lot of time on his hands." It took us close to a year to win back the credibility and acceptability that we had had with this client.

During a recent question-and-answer period, I asked my class participants, "Do you regularly plan your sales contacts?" Here are a few of the anti-paperwork responses:

- "I don't have time. I have to make at least eight calls a day."
- "I usually feel my way around when I get in to see the client." (Not to be confused with an information-gathering, fact-finding call.)

- "I know my products inside out. I am there to sell."
- "I go through my catalogue. The client will stop me if he spots something interesting."
- "Plan a call? I haven't done it for 20 years; why start now?"
- "Why am I making this contact? Because it's March 15th, that's why."

OVERCOMING THE POTENTIAL BARRIER OF CROSSED VIEWPOINTS

To be able to present from the client's position, as he or she wishes to hear it, a salesperson must plan from the client's side of the table. The client's viewpoint is quite different from the salesperson's viewpoint:

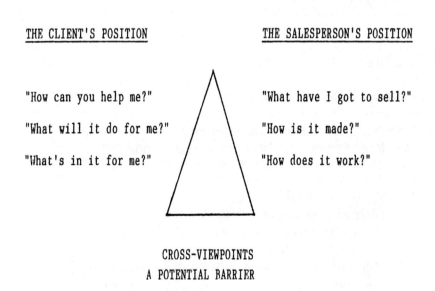

THE CLIENT'S POSITION   THE SALESPERSON'S POSITION

"How can you help me?"   "What have I got to sell?"

"What will it do for me?"   "How is it made?"

"What's in it for me?"   "How does it work?"

CROSS-VIEWPOINTS

A POTENTIAL BARRIER

With good planning and a little imagination, the salesperson can develop a selling blueprint (more on this subject later) that answers the client's questions in the left-hand column by converting the features and characteristics of the products or services in the right-hand column into client benefits:

"Mr. Smith, on my last call, you told me that you were looking for a way to increase your productivity and, at the same time, reduce the amount of scrap that you are losing. I have prepared this chart that will show you how you can achieve both of these goals with the features of our product."

PRE-CALL RESEARCH

Salespeople will be better prepared to make that first, all-important sales contact if they research the client and find out as much as possible about his business. Pre-call research takes some time and effort; however, it will really pay off when the first contact is made. Uncovering certain facts and information will provide the salesperson with areas to explore and will encourage the client to open up and talk. The client will recognize that the salesperson is concerned and interested in what is happening in the changing marketplace and, in particular, what the client's stake is in the scheme of things.

Information Sources to Research

- Dun and Bradstreet and other credit organizations.
- Dodge reports and other trade research groups.
- State directory of manufacturers.
- Association publications.
- Telephone and trade directories.
- Clubs and business organizations.
- Newspaper business sections.
- In-house resources.
- Other salespeople, through word-of-mouth.
- Eyes and ears.

I have been amazed how much one can learn by spending a couple of hours in the business section of the local library—and it's free!

PLANNING A FIRST-TIME FACT-FINDING CALL

To avoid hit-or-miss approaches, a salesperson can use a checklist to come up with areas to examine when the contact is made. Checklists are a boon to salespeople! They have a twofold value:

1. As a pre-call check when planning the call.
2. As a post-call check to evaluate what was, and what was not, achieved.

The salesperson may not use all of the factors listed at any given time. The checklist will make sure that important areas are not missed. A typical checklist follows.

A Call Plan Checklist

- What do they do? What business are they in?
- Who is their competition? Is the competitor a better prospect?
- Is their business healthy?
- What is their financial position?
- Are they growing?
- Are they aggressive?
- How do they go to market?
- How long have they been in business?
- What is their reputation in the marketplace?
- How many employees do they have?
- What is their employee turnover ratio?
- Is it a family business?
- Is there a sound line of succession in their management structure?
- Do I know the names and correct titles of key personnel? Can I pronounce their names properly?
- Who are the decision makers?
- Who are the key influencers?
- Am I planning to see the right person(s)?
- What do their clients think of their service? Go talk to them.

Now add your own points to the checklist:

-

-

-

-

-

-

With this information, the salesperson will be fully prepared to make that first, all-important sales contact. He or she will be able to generate two-way communication and uncover an area of need that can be resolved with the salesperson's products and/or services:

"Ms. Brown, I read in yesterday's newspaper that a major overseas company will be expanding operations into your trading areas. Do you feel that this is the right time to conduct the market analysis?"

If P.P. Perkins over at Mammoth used these planning techniques, he would probably be able to convert his enthusiastic non-users into enthusiastic users.

PLANNING A FOLLOW-UP SALES CONTACT

A specific objective must be established for this call. The salesperson has uncovered an area of need and will plan his objective based upon that need.

NEED→	NO AGREEMENT	NO SOLUTION→
←NO NEED	NO AGREEMENT	←SOLUTION
NEED→	AGREEMENT	←SOLUTION

My objective is to:

Help my client achieve an objective or meet a need.

↓

Uncover his or her goals/problems/concerns/applications.

↓

Provide the appropriate product or service that will help the client begin to benefit.

↓

Achieve trust, credibility, and commitment.

↓

Secure long-term worthwhile business relationships.

The old adage is just as applicable today as it was many years ago:

PROPER PRIOR PLANNING PREVENTS POOR PERFORMANCE.

PRACTICE EXERCISE: THE SALES CALL ACTION PLAN

How much do you really know about your prospects? Pick out a couple of tough ones and develop your own sales call action plan. (A sample plan is on the following page.) Use the balance of this page for any notes.

Notes

SALES CALL ACTION PLAN

Name of client contact_____ Date_____

_____

What do I need to know about my client's
business? How will I research the project?

_____

_____

_____

What is the purpose for my call?_____

_____

What client need does my purpose address?_____

_____

How will it benefit my client?_____

_____

_____

How have I prepared to make this sales call?_____

_____

How will I record the key information gathered?_____

_____

_____

What do I hope to achieve on this call?_____

_____

_____

What will be my fallback position if I do not attain my

first objective?_____

_____

_____

Other observations_____

_____

_____

_____

_____

A PLANNING CHECKLIST

Activities

- Good planning requires effort.
- Good planning requires the right attitude.
- Documents are tools that help the salesperson do a better job–not paperwork!
- Good planning produces worthwhile sales contacts.
- Planning is a necessary part of a productive selling strategy.
- Planning will eliminate hit-or-miss calls.
- Planning will help to overcome the barrier of crossed viewpoints (e.g., what it is vs. what it does).
- Develop selling blueprints by combining benefits and supportive features that address the client's needs.
- Pre-call research. Uncover facts and information that will provide subject areas to explore.
- Plan the first-time fact-finding call. Use a call plan checklist.
- Plan the follow-up sales contact. Establish a definite objective that will help the client begin to benefit.
- Use a sales call action plan.

Chapter 2

Preparing for a Productive Sales Call

Anticipation: Realization in advance. Expectation.

–The American College Dictionary

- I will prepare my sales presentation for delivery in the client's comfortable style of communication.

- I will anticipate my client's questions and requests and prepare to handle them when they do arise.

- I will take the time and make the effort to be sure that my supportive materials help rather than hinder me.

Preparation is defined as "to make ready; to furnish or equip with the necessary accessories." Part of my preparation in writing this book was to interview a number of buyers to get their opinion of the levels of preparation that they had observed in the salespeople who called on them. As the interviews progressed, I found myself becoming defensive; I wanted equal time to tell them what I thought buyers lacked in their own job preparation. After a while, I realized that part of my defensive posture was created because I was guilty of many of the points they had made.

The buyers' comments were both positive and negative:

- "He was well prepared–kept his brochures in folders to prevent them from becoming dog-eared."
- "He was disorganized–had to go out to his car to find a piece of literature."
- "She really had nothing of interest to show me–wanted to talk about the weather."

- "I got the impression that he was unprepared–fumbled around in his briefcase for something to talk about."
- "She couldn't find the right pages in the catalogue–seemed to be ill at ease."
- "He smothered me with information overload–I couldn't pick up the brochures fast enough."
- "He really got my interest. He showed me how I could increase my sales penetration of the market segment that we have targeted. He had an action plan that gave me a breakdown of potential sales by product and how we could achieve our market share–a real pro!"

A professional salesperson is always prepared to make each sales call a productive one. A salesperson who is not prepared, or who makes casual, no-purpose calls will lose the prestige and acceptance of himself and his organization.

I will always remember an ex-colleague of mine (now retired) who can best be described as having a chaotic approach to selling. Hap ("Hazard") Hayward is a tall, angular man given to loose-fitting dark suits. His colleagues often joked about his penchant for flying his trousers at half-staff–a reference to the fact that his pant cuffs were always about four inches above his shoe tops. He resembled a rumpled version of Abraham Lincoln, a fact not lost on Hap. On many occasions, his presentations were delivered as if they were the Gettysburg Address.

Hap disliked paperwork of any kind. He would load up his briefcase with a variety of flyers, brochures, catalogues–whatever happened to be available at the time. The trunk of Hap's car could be classified as a "garage sale" type of trunk–a beat-up profusion of samples, manuals, price books, catalogues, brochures, golf books, golf clubs, golf shoes, a baby buggy, and a cooler. Buyers had a special routine that they used on Hap. They called it the *Mission Impossible* ploy, wherein they would ask him for an obscure brochure and then continue working while Hap was in the parking lot frantically wading through the assortment in the trunk of his car.

Because of Hap's lack of preparation prior to his sales calls, he was constantly on the defensive. His sales contacts were of a general nature, with no real purpose. The buyer would come to the

Hap Hayward "self-destructing" in the customer's parking lot.

conclusion that his or her valuable time was being wasted and terminate the interview.

TO MAKE READY MEANS ANTICIPATING CLIENT REQUESTS

A very experienced salesman told me that a key part of his preparation is to put himself in the client's shoes and try to anticipate the client's reaction. He said that he visualizes the sales meeting taking place and then asks himself, "What questions or information would I want addressed if I were on the receiving end of this sales presentation?" In this way, he can prepare his briefcase with all of the material that will help him to answer the client's requests–on the spot! The key word here is *anticipation.*

Potential Client Questions/Requests

- "Do you have a brochure that details this operation?"
- "What data do you have to support your claims?"
- "Have you prepared a program overview and proposal?"
- "What are the time frames for each of these phases?"
- "How would your organization support us in this venture?"
- "How long would it take to get this project into production?"
- "Are you offering this package to anyone else in my trading area?"

Take a look at your own upcoming sales contacts. Can you anticipate the type of questions that you would have to address? How would you handle them?

Questions/Requests   **Response**

- •

- •

- •

- •

- •

The more I think about preparation, the more E.S. ("Eagle Scout") Gurley comes to mind. E.S. works for Mammoth Enterprises. I should explain that Mammoth is a large manufacturer of brass fittings. E.S. is a senior representative specializing in heavy industrial fittings. He is not a friend of P.P. Perkins.

"Be prepared at all times" is the motto of E.S. Gurley. He is well known at Mammoth for his profound observations, the most notable being: "A scruffy brochure is a scruffy brochure!" Another gem that I particularly like is: "An organized briefcase is a happy briefcase!"

E.S. is a methodical, organized person who leaves nothing to chance. He plans and prepares each sales contact as if it were a major battle plan. He believes in checklists and meticulously plans and prepares for each sales call with a definite objective in mind. He keeps excellent notes and, because he is genuinely interested in people, he is able to learn a lot about his clients and their business objectives and prepare his approach accordingly. His supportive aids are clear and concise, emphasizing the major points of his presentation.

TO MAKE READY MEANS PREPARING SUPPORTIVE AIDS

Supportive aids are just that–aids! They support, clarify, and augment the sales presentation, but they do not stand alone. They can focus attention on key points by dramatizing and enhancing these points. They prove that one picture is worth a thousand words. They can expand the educational process. They *do not* replace the salesperson.

Too many salespeople discuss a lengthy brochure or proposal without really knowing whether or not the client is following their line of thought. This is further complicated when the salesperson is sitting across from the client. The client is probably reading at his own speed or contemplating what he will have for dinner.

Good preparation will help the salesperson to guide the client's attention along a logical path.

- Brochures are wordy. Highlight or circle key points (particularly benefits) that are to be emphasized.

- Bullet or highlight major points in proposals and presentation material.
- Handouts should be clear, concise, easy to follow.
- Keep data, testimonials, and other documents brief and to the point.
- All slides, transparencies, charts, and other supportive material should be uncluttered with a minimum of verbiage. *Six lines* maximum per chart.
- Be brutal! Edit the material. Say it in one sentence rather than one paragraph.
- Don't let the client become a wide-awake sleeper.
- Ask this question of yourself: "If I hadn't seen this material before, could I fully understand and follow it as this salesperson is presenting it?"
- Get a colleague's opinion. Ask him how he would react to this material.

How about your sales presentation materials? Do they have a logical flow? Do they have a beginning, a middle, and a conclusion? Are they easy to follow? Are they uncluttered, concise, and *brief?* Do they really support what you intend to achieve? Have you avoided information overload? How could you improve them?

Supportive aids	Quality analysis	Improvements
1.		
2.		
3.		
4.		
5.		

TO MAKE READY MEANS ADAPTING
TO THE CLIENT'S STYLE OF OPERATION

People do business with people–*not* organizations. Since each client has a style of operating, build a comfortable climate for effective two-way communications. (The next chapter of this book covers the need to establish a comfortable business climate. We can *prepare* our approach and material to each client's comfortable operating style; therefore, I have positioned this pre-contact activity in the preparation chapter.) "Eagle Scout" Gurley has, as noted, a methodical approach to communicating. Each step is systematically laid out and supported with factual data. When he calls on a client who is *not* detail-oriented, who looks for bottom-line options, E.S. must *make adjustments* in his approach and sales presentation.

Each client tends to react differently when salespeople present their solutions and recommendations. Some people are assertive and others are more cautious in the decision-making process. Some are task- and time-oriented, make quick decisions, and care little about relationships. Others like to operate with people. They seek consensus decision making and require a comfortable business climate.

These human traits can cause misunderstandings, misinterpretations, and breakdowns in communications. When we recognize these differences and prepare our sales approach in the operating style of each client, we can establish a comfortable climate and, as a result, encourage active participation by the client.

Client style of operation	Preparing the approach
• *The decisive, "get it done" style* All business . . . blunt . . . to the point . . . time-oriented . . . no chit-chat . . . *motivated by achievements.*	Be specific . . . businesslike . . . avoid small talk . . . keep details to a minimum . . . don't use lengthy, cluttered materials . . . provide bottom-line options. . . Establish time frames.

Client style of operation	Preparing the approach

<table>
<tr><td></td><td>"Mr. Smith, regarding your new project: I have here option A and option B. I recommend that you consider option A and that we set it in motion the first of next month."</td></tr>
</table>

- *The persuasive, expressive "big picture" style*

Energetic . . . enthusiastic . . . does not like detail . . . enjoys conversation . . . *motivated by excitement.*	Encourage their enthusiasm . . . avoid excessive detail . . . take time to socialize . . . be a good listener . . . support the big picture and potential results.
	"Mr. Smith, within 18 months, you will be able to achieve the national market penetration that you want with this new program. I believe that it will have the same impact that you achieved last year with your revised distribution program."

- *The "team consensus" style*

Patient . . . group-oriented . . . team player . . . friendly . . . good listener . . . *Motivated by group cooperation.*	Be sincere . . . use open-end questions . . . give assurances . . . keep the climate comfortable . . . don't over-power or come on too strong.
	"Mr. Smith, with both teams working together under your direction, I know that you will be able to achieve the market penetration that you seek. Have I shown you how this total team concept will work for you?"

• *The "facts only please" style*

Methodical . . . detail-oriented
. . . likes organization . . .
wants testimonials . . .
motivated by accuracy.

Have all of the facts . . . be
well prepared . . . provide
proof . . . be specific . . . use a
logical, sequential flow.

"Mr. Smith, I have prepared
this three-phase flow chart
that will show you how you
can achieve the market
penetration that you want. In
addition, these industry
forecasts and statistics support
the percentage of market share
that we have projected."

I am not suggesting that a salesperson should try to change his or
her style. By simply *modifying the extremes* of one's own style to
make it *compatible* to the client's style and then preparing the presentation based upon the style requirement, each salesperson will be
able to build a communication bridge. As a result, the client will be
comfortable and more willing to participate in two-way communication. My style is expressive, outgoing, talkative. When I call on a
methodical, detail-oriented person, I present my recommendations in
an orderly, step-by-step fashion and keep my chatter under control.

Consider two or three of your own clients or prospects. Think
about those with whom you may have trouble communicating. How
would you prepare your approach and material?

What excesses of your own style could you modify to build your
communication bridge?

Client	Style	Your personal style modification activities
1.		
2.		

3.

4.

A PRE-CALL PREPARATION CHECKLIST

- Do I have a confirmed appointment? With the right person?
- Have I re-familiarized myself with the correct names, pronunciations, and titles of the people I will be contacting?
- Have I re-evaluated the purpose of my call?
- What specific client needs have I uncovered to date?
- What is the objective of this client? Am I addressing this objective?
- What are the prime advantages that my products and/or services solution can bring to the client?
- Have I anticipated logical responses to my proposal and thought through my solution?
- Have I adapted my approach to the comfortable operating style of my client?
- Have I organized my client's file in case quick reference is needed?
- Have I organized my briefcase?
- Are documents and papers arranged in good order?
- Are brochures and other literature up to date and clean?
- Is presentation manual clear and unmarked?
- Are notebook and business cards readily available? (A buyer told me that he is completely turned off when a salesperson makes notes on the back of an envelope or on scraps of paper.)
- Will I have readily available the samples, graphics, proposals, and other supportive aids that address the needs of the client?
- Am I prepared to remain conscious of the time allotted versus the material to be covered?
- Have I considered the commitment that I expect to get and the keys to receiving a positive response?

Others

-

-

-

Planning and preparing to make a sales contact go hand in hand. We start by defining our objectives for the call, as discussed in the previous chapter. If we ask ourselves, "What do I expect to achieve on this call?" we can prepare the necessary materials and approach prior to making the contact. A sales call to uncover needs, present a solution, or resolve a problem requires some degree of preparation. When the salesperson takes the time and makes the effort to develop a "preparation habit," the result will be better sales calls and presentations, and increased sales and profits.

A SELF-ANALYSIS CHECKLIST

Detail	Pre-call — Check each detail / Notes	Post-call — How well did I do? Well	Average	Needs work	Corrective action
Attitude. I will be:					
Positive					
Enthusiastic					
Open					
Concerned					
Receptivity. I will:					
Question					
Listen					
Show interest					
Be knowledgeable					
Preparation. I have my:					
Samples					
Literature					
Catalogues					
Proposals					
Visuals					

Chapter 3

Establishing a Comfortable Business Climate for Effective Two-Way Communications

Behavior: What a man does, not what he feels, thinks, or believes

–Benjamin C. Leeming

- I will recognize that the client is important and wants respect.

- I will build a comfortable communication climate for each of my clients.

- I will always project a professional image.

- I will remember that *how* I say and do things is as important as *what* I say and do.

- I will remember that people do business with people, not organizations.

The following are a few of the responses that I received from my buyer surveys regarding the various approaches used by salespeople:

"He comes on too strong."

"He tries to sit or stand too close to me."

"She doesn't look at me. I wonder if she really believes in what she is saying?"

"This particular salesman always wants to discuss sports, the weather, the world situation. Nice fellow! I wonder what he sells."

"She is a very good listener–shows real interest in what we are trying to do."

"I would describe her attitude as desperate–she must get through her spiel at all costs."

"The minute he sits down, he goes into his sales pitch–usually about a service for which we have no discernible need."

"I like the guy's approach. He is open, friendly, knowledgeable, and sincere. He is interested in what we are doing and he looks for ways that he can be of supportive value."

"This saleslady talks convincingly; however, her eyes–her expression–do not back up what she is saying."

"His delivery was mechanical–no warmth or feeling."

"He opened this massive catalogue and started to turn each page–I assume in the hope that I would recognize something of interest."

"She sat and looked at me. I imagine I was supposed to say something."

"I felt comfortable with her approach–low key and concerned."

From my buyer surveys, I also uncovered a number of comments that related to the ability of the salesperson to adjust their styles of communication to that of the buyer:

"He always has available the proof and documentation that I need." (A "facts only please" buyer.)

"I like the way that she gets right into the business discussion. There is no wasted time." (The decisive, "get it done" buyer.)

"He is always genuinely interested in my staff; they all like him, and work closely with him. My people work more effectively when they are comfortable with a supplier–that's important to me." (The "team consensus" buyer.)

"I like his enthusiasm for the project. He convinced my team that it will be fun working together, and this project requires close teamwork. Now I am caught up in it!" (The persuasive, expressive "big picture" buyer.)

A buyer told me that he likes to get to know the salesperson and his organization before he makes a favorable buying decision. He looks for the salesperson's interest in his objectives; sincerity; consistency; reliability, and, above all, an honest, straightforward approach. Many of the buyers disliked selling performances. One buyer commented that, "If I want to observe an actor at work, I will go to the theatre."

How we handle our first call on a prospect sets the stage for future business relationships with each client. When we are under pressure and our work load is heavy, we may be inclined to forget the importance of establishing and maintaining a comfortable business climate with each client. When we project a professional image at all times–when we show the client that we are interested in their well-being, and do everything that we can to help them meet their needs–we are establishing a comfortable business climate.

HOW THE CLIENT FEELS

Always remember these key points when dealing with a client:

- Clients do business with people, not organizations!
- The client feels that he is important.
- The client expects to be treated with respect.

Clients form first impressions. Although these first impressions are not always accurate, they can be long-lasting and, if negative, very difficult to overcome. How the client responds to the salesperson depends to a large degree upon the attitude and approach of the salesperson. A "know it all" approach–high-pressure tactics, a phony style, a defensive attitude–will turn off the client. The client will respond (positively or negatively) to *how* we say and do things. Most buyers are human beings; they like to talk about *their* concerns and needs, not the seller's.

One of my past assignments was to develop a long-term marketing action plan for a client. As part of my front-end-needs analysis research, I had the opportunity to sit in on a major presentation that my client made to one of their largest customers. This was a four-hour presentation conducted by an army of directors, vice presidents, and senior vice presidents. A very professional audio/visual, multi-projector approach was used. Unfortunately, the content was based upon in-house traditions. The product manager insisted upon having his hour on the program. The research and development people presented the latest in construction technology. Marketing Communications reviewed their latest strategies. Telecommunications planned to advise the customer on the latest innovations. The general manager planned to present policies and procedures. The senior vice president brought along his latest Rotary Club speech. As a result, the presentation devoured itself.

After a period of time, the president of the customer organization stood up and said, "Ladies and Gentlemen, you have been talking now for 38 minutes and 40 seconds. I have heard about your plant expansions, product innovations, market plans, and people. I have heard nothing about *our* needs and requirements." He then walked out. If my client's account executive had searched out the customer's goals and needs and then geared the presentation toward a solution, the presentation would have had less disastrous results.

HOW TO BUILD A COMFORTABLE BUSINESS CLIMATE TO FACILITATE THE SHARING OF IDEAS AND RECOMMENDATIONS

Attitude

The salesperson should develop, maintain, and project a positive, concerned, and interested attitude at all times. This is sometimes hard to do when working with a hard-to-please client. The salesperson may not always be able to get the client to like him; however, he must earn the client's respect. Remember that enthusiasm is contagious. (So is apathy and indifference.)

Always project an attitude of concern and interest in the client's needs and objectives. The salesperson must show a confidence and belief in himself, his company, its products and services, its people, and what this means to the client: The cup is always half full, not half empty.

The salesperson must feel good about himself and how he can be of value to the client. He should ask this question of himself, "What can I do today to help this client improve his or her situation?" Be a concerned, interested listener. (More on this key skill in the next chapter.) Don't play roles or silly games; our eyes are the mirrors to our thoughts. If we say one thing, and the client reads something different in our eyes, we will lose all credibility.

The Eyes May Not Have It

However skilled an actor a salesperson may think he or she is, one's real attitude will show in the eyes.

There are very few professional wide-awake sleepers in our business. These people probably hold a degree from a college that specializes in the mail-order business. They can actually maintain an expression in their eyes while sleeping.

When we don't pay attention, it's all there for the client to see. For instance, it is obvious when we practice selective listening–listening only to what we want to hear. Or when we pretend to listen, while thinking about what we want to say. Or when we lose concentration and start to drift or daydream. Our attitude, through our eyes, becomes one of indifference to the client's concerns, and he will read it.

PROJECT A PROFESSIONAL IMAGE

The time and effort put into planning and preparing sales calls will help to build a comfortable business climate. When the client is comfortable with us, we will have a much better chance to open up two-way communication and eliminate the possibility that the client will feel that he is being high-pressured or talked into something. In this way, we will be able to achieve the agreement and acceptance that we seek.

There is no way that anyone could convince Charlie ("Charger")

Chatham of this fact. Charlie had, somewhere along the way, decided that it was necessary to "charge the client," to make a big entrance and get "up close and personal" with the buyer. Charlie would purposefully march across the buyer's office, with a broad smile on his face and hand outstretched. He believed that to take charge, he must stand alongside the buyer and set up his presentation catalogue on the buyer's desk as he went into his routine (selling features, of course). Charlie possessed a large full-line catalogue, and because he represented Mammoth's brass binder division, his catalogue was generously edged in heavy brass.

Buyers are proud of their desks. In fact, a recent survey of 200 buyers showed that they would consider a new desk over all other awards as a suitable prize for a job well done. They soon realized that Charlie's brass-bound manual was hazardous to the health of desks in general, and they went to great lengths (stacking computer print-outs, etc.) to keep Charlie away. He had created a major barrier for himself. To this day, he puzzles over the fact that he is always seated as close as possible to the buyer's door. He had established an uncomfortable climate, and put the buyer on the defensive.

Sydney ("Superior") Swartz believed in an approach that was haughty and autocratic. His logic was that he must create the impression of possessing great knowledge and wisdom (excluding common sense) and that he would be willing to share this knowledge with a suitably impressed buyer and staff. He had no time for secretaries or receptionists–they were nuisance factors to be brushed aside as not worthy of his attention. He would majestically enter the buyer's kingdom and hold court. If other salespeople were waiting, they should be ignored as lesser subjects with no great message of wisdom. Not surprisingly, Sydney came across as a pompous ass. He can hardly get an appointment anymore. Buyers are usually "tied up at important meetings" when he calls.

Sydney Swartz majestically enters the buyers' kingdom to hold court.

Now Marv ("Modest") Miller had read somewhere that modesty is a becoming trait in a salesperson. Because his own comfortable style was friendly and considerate of other people, he felt that this was the right approach for him. He entered a client's office exuding an air of "forgive me for being here" to everyone involved. Reluctantly presenting his business card, he would retire to the farthest corner of the waiting room and await to be summoned. If he managed to reach the buyer, Marv would tentatively state, "I would like to be of help." He would then wait for the buyer to tell him how he could. The buyer, not really in a position to decide how Marv's products and services could be of value to him, closed out the meeting as quickly as possible. Marv had no purpose for his call and lacked confidence in himself and his sales ability.

The above salespeople had some good intentions, but they were playing roles. Over the years, I have been fortunate to work with many professional salespeople who have participated in my training workshops: At each session, we develop action plans that help us to define the skills that work at each step in the buyer/seller process.

One of the liveliest and most participative of these sessions is to build a checklist of skills that will help us all to establish a comfortable communication climate with each client. We usually agree that when we have built a comfortable, professional relationship with a client, we receive added value from the relationship:

- Ongoing sales (where appropriate).
- Valuable referrals–the power of word of mouth.
- Updated information on the industry or business.
- We keep our competitors out of the account.
- We develop close friendships that make both of us feel good about ourselves.
- We build productive, worthwhile, long-term business relationships.

AN EFFECTIVE TWO-WAY COMMUNICATIONS CHECKLIST

The following checklist is not complete by any means; we can always add new skills as we build our selling careers. However, the list does reflect the feelings and input of many professionals.

- Avoid selling performances or adopting an artificial veneer or style.

- Remember that the client is a human being and wants respect.

- Make the client's first impression a positive one.

- Be a concerned, interested listener. Encourage the clients to talk about their concerns and interests.

- Always keep the main purpose in focus: To help the client improve his or her situation. When we help the client gain, we gain.

- Be open and straightforward in all business dealings.

- *How* we say and do things is as important as *what* we say and do.
- Make sure that the eyes confirm what the mouth is saying.
- Let our natural style and, where appropriate, our sense of humor come through.
- Never become a wide-awake sleeper.
- Make operating style adjustments to match the clients. We should not attempt to change our own style; we must modify our own style excesses. If a salesperson's style is outgoing, boisterous, and talkative and he is working with a client who operates in a quiet, organized, and unemotional style, he must modify his approach. Excessive talking, a rousing joke, or boisterous laugh could turn off this client.
- We can further enhance the comfortable communications climate with each client if we recognize their style of operating and adapt to it.
- The confidence and belief that we have in ourselves, our company, its products and services, and its people will be reflected in how we relate to, and communicate with, our clients.
- We are in a profession that gives us an opportunity to help others. Let that natural enthusiasm shine through.
- We should ask ourselves these questions often: "Is this right for my client and my company? Is it a win-win situation?"

I can think of no better example of the effective use of these skills than those used by the following salesman. One of my clients hired a young salesman to open a new territory in the Seattle area. The man had sold for two years in a different business and had completed four weeks of in-house and on-the-job training. His competitor had a veteran salesman in the territory who was a real professional. Over the years, this veteran had built a fine reputation with the major distributors in the area and always conducted himself in a businesslike manner.

For 18 months, my client's salesman picked up the small amount of business to be found in the outlying areas of the territory. He could not sign a major distributor. Two years from the time that he moved into the territory, the competitor's veteran salesman retired. Six months later my client's salesman signed two major distributors to a contract.

I wish that I could have recorded all of the comments that were made by the senior buyer of one of the distributors. At the sales meeting kick-off, he told us that for two years our salesman had called on him regularly. He said that the salesman was always interested in what they were doing, was always cheerful, brought in current changes and developments that were happening in the industry; represented his company professionally; made some very good suggestions for market penetration; and was always ready to put himself out to help them. The buyer finished by saying, "We look forward to working with him." Today, this salesman is successful and a real asset to his company.

PRACTICE EXERCISE:
BUILD A COMFORTABLE RELATING ZONE

After you have had a chance to review the previous checklist, consider some of your tough clients:

- What barriers exist that adversely affect good two-way communications?

Barriers	Solutions
1.	1.
2.	2.
3.	3.

- What communication barriers do you create? Are you a selective listener, for example?

Self-inflicted barriers   **Your corrective actions**

Chapter 4

Uncovering Client Needs/Concerns/Applications

Silence: The space surrounding every action and every communion of people.

−Dag Hammarskjöld

- To uncover my clients' needs, I will encourage them to talk about their business and their people.

- I will ask the right type of questions to facilitate two-way communication.

- I will check understanding and acceptance at each step in the negotiating process.

- I will listen–really listen–to what my clients have to say.

- I will document important information before it slips away.

We salespeople are talkers, not listeners! We would rather tell you than ask you. The other day, I was waiting for an automobile salesman friend of mine and I happened to be standing next to a hearse. A salesman came up to me and said, "It's available! And I can get you a good deal." I told him that "I am not ready to go yet."

Considering the fact that we are good talkers and are knowledgeable about our company and its products and services, it is easy to see how the *cross-viewpoint barrier* can arise. We noted earlier that there is a potential cross-viewpoint barrier between the client's negotiating position and the salesperson's position:

The client	**The salesperson**
• I have needs and objectives.	• This is what I have to sell.
• Can you help me? I want a solution.	• This is how it is made.
• How will I benefit?	• This is how it works.

Cross viewpoint is a tough barrier to overcome. We work hard at learning as much as we possibly can about our products and services, which is an important part of our job. We are not trained in the skills of evaluating how our products and services meet a client need. The situation I mentioned earlier in which the president of my client's customer organization walked out of a major presentation is a typical example of a supplier merely presenting a product, mistakenly assuming that the customer could relate these features and details to an objective of his own.

Betty ("Boom Boom") Brasher of Mammoth tries to *sell* products: "Mr. Goodbuyer, this new brass unit has an excellent dual-rotary hinge, tungsten-carbide louvres, and is available in standard and custom-designed packages. What do you think?"

"About what?"

"This new unit. It was two years in development and required a considerable amount of investment to reach its present state-of-the-art level. We at Mammoth Enterprises are very proud of it."

"That's very nice. What did you say your name was again?"

"Betty Brasher."

"Well, Ms. Brasher, it is comforting to know that everyone at Mammoth is getting a warm feeling over this unit. Now if you will excuse me I must prepare for a management meeting scheduled for 15 minutes from now. Goodbye!"

Betty had talked only from the seller's side of the table.

HOW TO SEARCH OUT THE CLIENT NEEDS

Effective negotiated selling in any business situation is the result of mutual discussion and the exchange of thoughts, ideas, and recommendations that lead to agreement and acceptance. To uncover potential areas of need–to arouse the client's interest in a solution–we salespeople must be skilled in the effective use of *two* essential tools for productive two-way communication:

1. The ability to ask the right type of questions
2. The ability to really listen to the responses

These two skills are perhaps two of the most important tools that we can carry in our "tool bag." I have found that this is not always the thinking of the salespeople who participate in my workshops:

- "I am there to sell, not to encourage a friendly discussion."
- "I have the best product in the business, at a competitive price. My job is to sell the buyer."
- "Letting my clients ramble eats into my selling time; it's short enough as it is."
- "Usually my clients don't know what they need; it's up to me to show them."
- "If I let them take charge of the discussion, I will probably lose."

It is interesting to note that in each of these statements the salespeople involved are advocating *one-way* communication.

As a business consultant, marketing/sales specialist, and trainer, I sell intangibles; I have no actual product to sell. I must find a need before I can evaluate whether or not my services can provide a solution. I have found that a five-question checklist approach will encourage discussion and provide me with a client area of need to explore.

A NEEDS ANALYSIS CHECKLIST

1. "What are your primary objectives for your sales team?"
   "What stands in the way of achieving these objectives?"
2. "What do you expect from your salespeople?"
3. "What are their strengths?"

4. "What areas need improvement?"

5. "What has been done in the past to address these needs?"

Your Needs Analysis Checklist. What Questions Do You Use to Get the Information That You Need?

1.

2.

3.

4.

5.

ASK THE RIGHT TYPE OF QUESTIONS TO GET THE CLIENT TO OPEN UP

The Ice-Breaker Question

This is a friendly greeting that bridges into the business discussion. Referring back to the comfortable operating styles of people, there are those who would want to take time to chitchat a bit and would expect us to adjust accordingly. These people look for an ice-breaker approach. Pick a general subject of mutual interest, preferably one that is related to the client's field of interest:

- "Mr. Smith, I noticed that you have expanded your recreation facilities since my last visit."
- "Ms. Brown, I read your very interesting article in last month's journal."

What ice-breaker questions do you use? Do you use them with the relationship-oriented people?

1.

2.

3.

With an ice-breaker, we must be sincere or we will come across as phony. If we don't carefully listen to the response, this could happen:

"Mr. Smith, how are you today?"

"Terrible! I have a headache!"

"Super! Now let me tell you what I have for you today."

Instant loss of credibility!

The Open-End Question

An open-end question is used to encourage elaboration by the client. Open-end questions *do not* limit the client's response to a *yes or no* answer and are used when the client is willing, or able, to give us the information that we need. An open-end question begins with What, Why, How, When, or Who:

- "*What* did you have in mind?"
- "*Why* is that?"
- "*How* do you plan to go about it?"
- "*When* will you be expanding?"
- "*Who* will head the project?"

The Directive Closed-End Question

A directive closed-end question is used to confirm a fact or agreement and to *direct* the discussion into areas to explore when the seller is not getting the information that he or she needs. We are digging for an area of need, *limiting* the client's response to a yes or no answer. A closed-end question begins with Have, Is, Will, or Would:

- *"Have* you made a decision?"
- *"Is* competition a major concern?"
- *"Will* you want immediate action?"
- *"Would* this be what you had in mind?"

In the planning chapter, we noted that it is to our advantage to plan the types of questions to use, especially on initial or fact-finding calls. There are appropriate questions that can be used with different industries and businesses. The five-question checklist that I used earlier consisted of open-end questions; however, if I did not get the response that I needed, I could switch to closed-end questioning or a combination of both.

Two salespeople in an automobile dealer showroom–Walter and Carl–take different approaches to a prospect. Walter tries to sell a product; Carl asks questions to uncover the prospect's interests and needs.

Walter spots a prospect and his family standing alongside a new model coupe:

"Nice-looking car," Walter says.

"Yes."

"Look at the equipment on this car–everything that you could want: spaciousness, real leather, four-speaker stereo. That's luxury!"

"So is the price."

"And worth every penny. We can give you a real nice discount and very low interest rates over four years. I would jump at it if I were you; it won't last long."

"I am sure that you are right; however, I am not in a jumping mood. Just looking. If I see a car that is suitable, I will have you hop on over."

Carl also sees a family looking at a particular model:

"Hello! I am Carl Colson. I imagine with all of the makes and models on the market today, it isn't easy to shop for a car. Did you have a car in mind to accommodate the whole family?"

"I am Fred Manning. Sure! As you can see there are enough of us."

"Mr. Manning, I see that you have a four-door car now. Is that still your preference?"

"Definitely! You haven't seen our dogs."

"Did you have a larger model in mind? And how about accessories?"

"What I am really thinking of is a four-door wagon with a V6 engine and no fancy accessories. I would think that power steering, automatic, air, and an AM/FM radio would be plenty for our needs."

"Mr. Manning, there are two models here that I believe will meet your needs. Your family and your dogs will have plenty of room. If you will come over here, I can show them to you."

Carl has uncovered a need and is starting to develop a solution. He could be on his way to making a sale.

Questions That Are Geared to a Specific Industry

A Bank Prospect

- "Do your branch managers and calling officers make regular sales calls?"
- "Are your trust officers and inside sales staff asking for the business?"
- "Can they cross-sell?"
- "Are you training them now in these skill areas?"

A Tire Dealer

- "What make and model of car do you drive?"
- "How many miles a year do you drive?"
- "What type of driving do you do? Highway? In town? All-terrain?"

- "What type of tires do you have on your car now?"
- "How long do you plan to keep your car?"

A Heating and Cooling Contractor

- "How long have you had your present furnace?"
- "Have you had your present furnace for about 15 years?"
- "Do you find the air in your house to be dry?"
- "Do you feel that your energy bills are too high?"

An Internal Needs Analysis

In this case, a department manager talking to an accounting systems manager who is using a manual accounting system:

- "How many invoices are processed a month?"
- "How many staff people are tied up in this activity?"
- "How many man-hours are involved?"

What Types of Open- and Closed-End Questions Do You Use in Your Business to Get the Information That You Need?

1.

2.

3.

4.

5.

6.

7.

Salespeople must use good judgment when using directive closed-end questioning. We must guard against coming across as too inquisitive or too aggressive. Avoid putting the client on the defensive. For example, Betty Brasher would have had more success with Mr. Goodbuyer if she had used the questioning approach:

"Mr. Goodbuyer, I read in the trade journal that you are planning to introduce a new line of top-quality cabinets and furniture. When do you expect to start tooling up for this line?"

"Probably by the end of the year."

"I see. My reason for asking is that we have made quality brass hinges for some of the finest cabinet manufacturers, at a competitive price. Our other clients say they have had virtually no problems with our fittings and that our service has been very reliable."

"We would be interested in testing your product in our upcoming test runs. Get back to me in about four weeks and we will set it up."

CHECKING UNDERSTANDING AND ACCEPTANCE TO ENSURE AGREEMENT AT EACH STEP IN THE NEGOTIATION PROCESS

The Check Question

At this stage in the negotiative selling process, we *check* certain facts or details during the two-way communication flow. To be sure there is clear understanding on the part of both parties involved, points are qualified and/or clarified. Is the buyer really accepting what the seller is offering? Is the seller assuming that the client is "buying into" his recommendations? A rule of thumb is that if the salesperson talks for three minutes or more, *stop* and *check* the client's understanding and acceptance. The salesperson may have a wide-awake sleeper on his hands. Take heed, all of you energetic talkers!

When we are involved in a lengthy discussion, particularly where a lot of data or detail is discussed, stop and give the client a chance to catch up. *Save his face* to prevent him from becoming defensive: "Mr. Smith, I have covered a lot of ground so far and done a lot of talking. Have I presented this material clearly?" Involving the client in the decision-making process eliminates the hard sell and encourages the *we* rather than *you* or *I* during the negotiation. There is another old saying that is still true today: He who listens well is always popular and eventually learns something!

If the automobile salesman had asked me some key questions and listened to my responses, he may have sold me that hearse, although I doubt it:

- "Perhaps you could use the hearse when you are making your sales calls. The client would be intrigued and probably recognize that you need an order! What do you think?"
- "There is a six-speaker stereo system on board that would provide suitable music during the journey. Do you feel that this would be desirable?"
- "Mr. G., you would like to go out in style, wouldn't you? (Just kidding.)"

EFFECTIVE LISTENING

Effective listening involves giving attention for the purpose of *listening to* and *absorbing* information. Without attention and awareness, there is only a mechanical translation of the spoken word.

```
┌─────────────────────┐
│                     │
│      ABSORB         │
│                     │
│      RETAIN         │
│                     │
│      RECALL         │
│                     │
└─────────────────────┘
```

Absorb key information through careful listening and appropriate note-taking.

Retain key information with detailed notes in a suitable file.

Recall key information when it is required.

With effective listening techniques, a salesperson can use past information to create future sales: "Mr. Smith, way back in March you mentioned that you would be looking at an expansion program in about six months' time. Is that project coming up soon?" Be a concerned, interested listener! Good listening requires concentration! Good listening requires attention!

HOW TO REALLY LISTEN TO–RATHER THAN HEAR– WHAT THE CLIENT IS SAYING

Effective listening cannot be a contrived action. Listening only to those points that are of interest to the seller, or tuning out the client as he or she talks, will be spotted immediately, and the salesperson will lose any two-way communication that has been developed.

To my knowledge, no woman has ever given birth to an effective listener. Effective, *active* listening is a skill that has to be learned and constantly practiced to be truly productive. Any professional mind reader worth his turban learns right away to develop the skills of active listening and storing of names and places.

Have you ever had the experience of meeting someone for the first time and then five minutes later you can't remember his or her name? We then spend a lot of time "waltzing around," hoping that someone will drop the other person's name. Isn't it interesting that the other person almost always seems to remember ours? Could it be that we are so busy thinking about what *we* want to say that we fail to listen? Could it be that we are distracted by our thoughts: "I wouldn't be seen *dead* in that outfit" or "Why does he have a paper clip stuck on his lapel?"

Recently, I was a guest speaker at a realtor's convention. During a break, the subject of effective listening came up. A very successful realtor rated herself a ten (the only one that I have ever met–at least pertaining to listening). She talked about *total concentration* and proceeded to review the major points that I had covered to that time, and she was right on! I was impressed. That evening, I was explaining to my wife how effective this lady had been, and my wife asked me her name. I couldn't remember! So it's practice time again.

Most experts agree that effective negotiative selling from the client's position is approximately two-thirds questioning and listening and one-third talking. It is clear that salespeople must be proficient at both of these skills. When the salesperson listens–really listens–to the client's needs and objectives, when he is a concerned and interested listener, he shows the client that *his* interests are also the salesperson's interests.

By being a good listener, the salesperson builds, in the client's eyes, the prestige of himself as well as the organization that he represents. Try the evaluation below and test your listening skills.

A PERSONAL LISTENING SKILLS EVALUATION

SKILL	ALMOST NEVER	RARELY	OFTEN	ALMOST ALWAYS
I make a point of remembering names, titles, and other important details.	____	____	____	____
I document this information.	____	____	____	____
I concentrate on the core (meaning) of what is said.	____	____	____	____
I concentrate physically and mentally.	____	____	____	____
I listen for key clues that will help me to uncover a client need.	____	____	____	____

A PERSONAL LISTENING SKILLS EVALUATION

SKILL	ALMOST NEVER	RARELY	OFTEN	ALMOST ALWAYS
I key in on what is being said not how it is said.	___	___	___	___
I look for non-verbal signals to help me to develop the right response.	___	___	___	___
I work at blocking out distractions that may interfere with my concentration.	___	___	___	___
When I ask a question I listen to the response.	___	___	___	___
I think about what I am going to say while the other person is talking.	___	___	___	___
I make a point of not interrupting the other person until he has finished speaking.	___	___	___	___

A PERSONAL LISTENING SKILLS EVALUATION

SKILL	ALMOST NEVER	RARELY	OFTEN	ALMOST ALWAYS
I am a <u>concerned</u>, <u>interested</u>, listener, and show the people with whom I communicate that their interests are my interests.	____	____	____	____
I try not to get my message across too quickly, and hear the other person out.	____	____	____	____
I make a point of staying alert when the other person is talking.	____	____	____	____
I put a real effort into acquiring good listening habits.	____	____	____	____

Others

•

•

•

Corrective Action

Select the one or two listening skills that are your weakest. Decide upon the corrective action you will take. For example, I tend to interrupt. To help me better hear out the client, I place reminder notes over my car visor, in my briefcase, and in my presentation material. If you try to get your message across too quickly, try making reminder notes at certain points in your script that will act as red flags as you proceed. Then at the end of the week, review your achievements. Select another listening skill and build your *action plan* that will help you to correct it. Recognizing an area that needs improvement and then *taking action* to correct it will help you to improve your listening skills.

Skill   **Action Plan Steps**   **Review**

A final word about listening.

Throughout this book, I have stressed the importance of being a concerned, interested listener. Yet we cannot pretend to listen! It will show every time. I have been married for 40 years, and I have learned the difficult skill of being able to grunt in the right places when my wife talks to me while I am reading the newspaper. On occasion, I can even give a reasonable answer in the correct sequence. I call this "two-dimensional attention." The other day I had a rude awakening when my wife said, "You aren't fooling anyone. When you pretend to listen you get that glazed look in your eyes. Haven't I heard you talk about the eyes reflecting what the mouth is saying?" As a result, I have lowered my listening skills rating from a 6 to a 5.5.

Chapter 5

Presenting the Solution from the Client's Needs Position

> Creativity: It is not the finding of a thing, but the making something out of it after it is found.
>
> –James Russell Lowell

- I will remember that the only thing that I have to sell is client benefits.

- I will support my client benefits with the appropriate features/details/characteristics of my products or services.

- I will use all of my company's attributes that produce value for my client.

- I will compare my products and services with the competitors, while searching out the advantages my products and services offer the client that my competitor does not have available.

- I will present my solution in a clear, concise, easy-to-understand manner from my client's viewpoint.

We have reached the stage in the selling process where the salesperson has uncovered a client need or objective, planned and prepared the solution, and is ready to present it to the client. The client will buy what the product or service will *do* for him or her, not *what* it is or *how* it is constructed. The presentation must answer the client's question: "What will it do for me, my company, or my people?" Therefore, the only thing that we have to sell is benefits-client benefits! Everything else is supportive–necessary but supportive. Remember the client's point of view:"Don't try to sell me your products and services; help me to buy what I need. Show me an action plan that will produce better results than I am now getting and I will be interested."

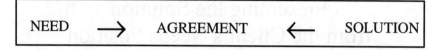

NEED $\longrightarrow$ AGREEMENT $\longleftarrow$ SOLUTION

Client benefits sell. The relative features of a product or details of a service are the source of client benefits. There is a definite *cause/ effect* relationship between the two.

WHAT IS A BENEFIT?

A benefit is the *tangible result* that the client receives from a product or service. Action verbs are "trigger words" that tell the client it is a benefit:

INCREASE	DECREASE	IMPROVE
EXPAND	DELETE	SAVE
DEFINE	ELIMINATE	REDUCE

These trigger words can be used in either statement or question form:

- "Mr. Smith, *you can increase* your rate of productivity . . ."
- "Mr. Smith, *if I can show* you how you can *increase* your rate of productivity . . . "

I suppose everyone knows benefit selling–including Bo! What is surprising is how benefits are used or, rather, how they are not used.

Pick up any company's literature and look for client benefits. You will have no trouble finding features and details–lots of them. As a rule, company literature is written by in-house marketing/advertising people from the seller's side of the table.

Mammoth's Bill ("Benefits") Jones is one of the most knowledgeable salesmen I know. He systematically lists every product and service that Mammoth offers and then develops the relative features of the product or details of the service. His next step is to take *each* feature or detail and build *all* of the *benefits* that *relate* to each one. Then, when the client states, "I am interested in safety right now, not profit," Bill brings up those benefits and features that address the client's *current* need. Bill loves benefits! He is known affectionately as "Captain Benefits" and has a cap (gold braid and all) to prove it. He figures that his cap is worth five strokes on the golf course. Some people say that he wears underclothes that carry the slogan "Benefits supported by features." Of course, this could just be idle gossip.

Bill is a very successful salesman. He has developed a "tool bag" of benefits, features, and details. Once he has established the client's specific need, he pulls out those tools that help him to develop a solution to the need.

If I were selling industrial equipment and the plant engineer said, "My real concern right now is safety; we have a poor safety record," I would go to my tool bag and pull out those benefits and features that relate to safety. There would be no purpose for me to talk profit at this time. His mind is on one thing–safety. I would say: "Mr. Smith, I can understand your concern. I am sure that safety is a major concern of all plant engineers and superintendents. To *protect* against accidents, *reduce* the possibility of employee injury, and maintain a *good* safety record for our clients, we paint all key areas with easy-to-see yellow paint and place protective shields over all moving parts." The value of *preparing* selling blueprints makes this switch possible.

Benefit/Feature Analysis Practice

Some of the following statements are benefit statements and some are feature/detail statements. The feature/detail statements are followed by the client's thoughts in parentheses.

1. "Ms. Brown, our follow-up service is the finest in the industry." (This is an opinion and probably debatable.)
2. "Mr. Jones, we give you a three-year warranty when you buy this unit from us." (A piece of paper–tell me what it will do for me.)
3. "Mr. Green, our new computer can definitely *reduce your investment* in inventory and *speed up* delivery service in the bargain."
4. "Ms. Wilson, have I shown you how it is possible to *reduce eye strain* with this new screen?"
5. "Mr. Gold, there are eight safety shields on this new piece of equipment." (So what! How will my people be protected?)
6. "Mr. Black, look at this: two reverse transverse keys, vertical stability and integrity, plus an instant release drop carriage." (A bunch of details! So what?)

BUILD SELLING BLUEPRINTS BY COMBINING BENEFITS AND FEATURES OR DETAILS

Unfortunately, a great number of business people confuse benefits and supportive features and, as a result, misuse them in a selling situation. To offset this problem, it is to the salesperson's advantage to develop selling blueprints *ahead of time.*

Each feature or detail can produce a number of benefits, with one benefit building on another: "Mr. Smith, your salespeople will be able to free up *more* discretionary selling time and make more *productive* sales contacts as a result of this practical training workshop. In addition, they will *increase* their close ratio, resulting in *more* sales, profits, and return on investments."

Benefits That Appeal to Emotion

A salesperson can develop benefits that appeal to the client's emotions if the solution warrants this approach. These emotional benefits include:

- Comfort
- Safety

- Protection
- Peace of mind
- Avoiding frustration

The selling blueprints address emotion, logic, or a combination of both, as we will see in the six-year warranty, automated teller service, and vinyl shade examples that follow.

Benefits That Appeal to Logic

A salesperson can develop benefits that appeal to the client's logic if the situation warrants this approach. These benefits include:

- Saving time and/or money
- Reducing downtime
- Increasing productivity
- Avoiding costly delays

When a selling blueprint containing all of the emotional and logical benefits is prepared ahead of time, the salesperson will be able to bring out any combination of benefits that will answer the client's needs. He now has a storyboard for his actual presentation.

Short- and Long-Term Benefits

As a salesperson becomes increasingly proficient at building selling blueprints, he or she can develop short-term benefits that lead into long-term benefits:

Expand market penetration → Broaden the customer base→ Increase market share → Attain long-term sales and profit objectives

Review the selling blueprint examples that follow, then develop you own on page 64.

SELLING BLUEPRINTS

To build a selling blueprint for any product or service, the salesperson develops
three factors:

PRODUCT/SERVICE FEATURE	ADVANTAGE/FUNCTION	CLIENT BENEFITS
Co-op advertising program.	Supplier will pay a co-op advertising allowance based upon a % of annual purchases.	Additional money available for more promotional activities. Improve cash flow.
A six year warranty.	Repairs can be handled at any location free of charge.	Save money. Eliminate downtime. Avoid frustration. Peace of mind.
Automated teller service.	More convenient. Cash is available when needed.	Save time and frustration. Avoid embarrassment. Peace of mind.

SELLING BLUEPRINTS

PRODUCT/SERVICE FEATURE	ADVANTAGE/FUNCTION	CLIENT BENEFITS
A shade with a vinyl inner layer.	Keeps heat in during the winter months and reduces heat penetration in the summer months.	Enjoy comfort in winter and summer. Reduce heating and cooling costs. Assures privacy.
Assured quality control.	Maintain and improve product life.	Reduce downtime. Less scrap and wastage. Improve plant profitability. Satisfied customers.
Your Selling Without Confrontation reference book.	Periodical review. Proven skills available for study and use.	More productive sales calls. Increased sales and profits. A happy boss.

SELLING BLUEPRINTS

PRODUCT/SERVICE FEATURE	ADVANTAGE/FUNCTION	CLIENT BENEFITS

This is the power of the selling blueprint concept. Try it for yourself. Go back and review the selling blueprints that you have just developed. What emotional and logical benefits have you noted? What benefits can you *extend* to long-term benefits? How can you use the emotion and logic benefits in tandem to produce your strongest storyboard?

Notes

Benefits for the Client and Others in Whom He Is Interested

A further extension of the selling blueprint approach is to develop benefits for the client's own customers, if this is called for. For example: If I am selling a product to a building developer who is in the process of planning to build a high-rise apartment building, my approach will be based upon whether or not he plans to keep or sell the building. If he plans to sell the building, my benefits would be geared toward helping him make the sale. If he plans to keep and operate the building, my benefits would include attracting the right tenants and maintaining a high tenant ratio. I would also build tenant benefits, such as a prestige area, year-round comfort, and complete security.

There are some situations that make it tough to develop benefits; however, they are there if we look for them. Try converting the following features/details into as many emotional and logical benefits as you can. Be as creative as you wish.

Features/Details	Benefits (E = Emotion; L = Logic)
A. "This price increase will take effect 60 days from today."	1.
	2.
	3.
	4.
B. "The co-op advertising allowance will be based upon less Yellow Page advertising and more on the use of broader media."	1.
	2.
	3.
	4.
C. "Field sales managers will now spend a minimum of three days a week in the field training their people."	1.
	2.
	3.
	4.
D. "This product has met and exceeded all of the Environmental Protection Agency standards."	1.
	2.
	3.
	4.

INTERNAL SELLING

These skills are equally effective internally when the client is the boss, department manager, or any other in-house person. We will have a much better chance of selling the boss on a change in marketing strategy if we develop a selling blueprint that projects the *added value* of the change.

A COMPANY ATTRIBUTE BLUEPRINT

Every organization or business has many resources that are the foundation upon which to build client benefits. When we discuss the price objection in my training workshops (more on this subject later), we invariably recognize the value of a company attribute blueprint. The client is really saying, "What am I getting for my money?" We ask ourselves, "Is my client really comparing apples to apples?" or "What do we have to offer that brings *added value* to the negotiating table?"

We search out such company attributes as:

- People value
- Reliability
- Delivery
- Consistency
- Support
- Reputation
- Quality

A company attribute blueprint will provide *additional sources* for client benefits.

An Attributes File

Company Attributes, Features,
<u>Characteristics, and Details</u>   <u>Potential Client Benefits</u>

- Company history and track record.
- Company reputation.
- Company stability.
- The strength of management.
- Stability of policy.
- Marketing policies and procedures.
- Client support.
- Products and/or services strengths.
- Product quality.
- Technical growth and commitment.
- Service support.
- Customer relationships and communications.
- People: Stability, concern, training, experience, interest, morale, and professionalism.

<u>Others (develop your own)</u>

-
-
-
-
-

We can produce powerful selling blueprints if we understand everything that the company has to offer and what this means to the client.

PRESENTING FROM THE SELLING BLUEPRINT

We noted that selling blueprints are the foundations for our sales talks. When the client has a need or objective that we can resolve, we pull out the appropriate blueprint, update it where necessary, and use it as our presentation format by working across the blueprint columns in our own selling style. There is a further step that we can take if we feel that the client will compare our offering with others available.

COMPARATIVE ANALYSIS

We all make comparisons:

* Should I go to bed or stay up and watch the late movie?
* Should I put $700 in the old car or go for a new one?
* Should I play golf or cut the grass?
* Should I take my spouse to the Waldorf Astoria or McDonalds for dinner?

Clients also compare:

* Does this supplier's past track record compare with my present one?
* How well does he support his claims compared with my present source?
* How well does his bid compare with the competitor's?
* What has he got to offer that my present supplier does not?

Because clients do compare, the salesperson has the responsibility to make sure that the client is comparing apples with apples. The client needs to know exactly what he is getting for his money. For many years I was involved in bid activity, and I eventually realized that a number of clients didn't fully understand how each bid compared with others in regard to value. They would look at the bottom-line cost without comprehending that one bid may lack a significant service compared with another. It became obvious just how valuable a company attributes list could be as an educational tool. I increased my number of successful bids when I did four things:

1. I would draw from my company attributes file all of the added-value factors that supported my price.
2. Whenever possible, I would sit down and educate the client as to what exactly he was getting for his money: "Mr. Smith, I know there are a lot of details to be considered when you evaluate these four bids. You will notice that we include (warranty, delivery, installation, training, etc.) at no extra cost. You may want to check out these additional services in your other bids. We believe that it is important to spell out, up front, exactly what you are getting, in order to offset later add-on costs."
3. I presented benefits supported by features, details, and testimonials. I wanted the client's mind on *value*, not financial outlay.
4. I found out everything that I could about my competitors–their strengths and lesser values. I would build a balance sheet of strengths and lesser values *comparisons.*

I did not win all of the bids, but I did get my share. I would never knock my competitor. I can compare product features and service details and stress the added value that I have to offer over my competitor. If my competitor had more benefits in a specific area, I would come back with other strengths taken from my file.

When we prepare a comparative balance sheet, we force ourselves to evaluate what we are up against. Although we may not use the right-hand side of the following balance sheet at all times, we are better prepared to use the left-hand columns. How well do you know your competitor? Can you hold your own in a comparative analysis session?

Comparative Balance Sheet

<u>Your Product/Service</u>   **<u>The Competitor's Product/Service</u>**

Strengths   *Lesser Values*   *Strengths*   *Lesser Values*

In summary, I am not advocating a canned presentation. We still need two-way communication, open discussion, and the sharing of ideas and recommendations. We must be alert to any new approaches that may surface during the discussion. The blueprints that have been documented here give us a track to follow, to help us to present from the client's viewpoint–from his side of the negotiating table. The client will recognize that we are presenting a solution to a need or concern, and not just trying to sell him something. We are eliminating the possibility of confrontation in the negotiating process. Every client is defensive and on guard against being sold. When we are in a store and a clerk asks us, "Can I help you?" we fall back on the "just looking" line of defense. People go car shopping on a Sunday because there are no salespeople ready to pounce.

My old, trusty word processor is closing in on the well-worn stage. A few days ago, I visited a large store that had a long line of modern word processors on display, stretching from the lowest priced model on the left to the *Star Wars* model on the right. I suddenly realized that I had positioned myself next to the lowest priced model. The salesclerk wasn't going to get me down to the other end. The client will become cautious when he feels that we are trying to sell him what we want to sell, rather than a solution to his needs. We must persuade and convince our client to buy. Our persuasive story, if based upon the client's needs, will reduce defensiveness and open up the two-way communications process–and that's what selling is all about!

THE PHYSICAL PRESENTATION

One of my buyer contacts told me that the sales presentations he had endured (his word) ranged from average to mediocre. Think back to the sales presentations in which you have participated, either as a presenter or a listener. Which ones do you remember–the effective ones or the bad?

When I reviewed my notes prior to writing this chapter, I found that I had made far more notes on the poor presentations than on the good ones:

- Non-directional rambling
- Nervous, distracting gestures
- Fumbling with script or visuals
- Muttering
- Haphazard wandering
- Falling off the stage (honest!)
- Dropping stuff on the floor

These and other distracting activities will be observed and noted by the listener or audience. The feeling is that if this presenter is insecure and uncertain, how can he or she expect me to buy into his ideas or recommendations? I actually watched a man walk across a stage toward the podium swinging his left arm and left leg in unison–try it some time. All of these nervous, distracting habits can be overcome with practice. There really is no substitute for practice!

The sales presentation that has the most positive impact upon the client is the one in which the presenter radiates confidence and *genuine* enthusiasm. Confidence is contagious–so is apprehension!

Confidence comes from having a good story to tell and being

able to present it effectively. The salesperson knows *how* to present it and is comfortable doing so. The salesperson has *practiced* and *timed* the presentation. The salesperson has *visualized* the flow of the presentation: It has a beginning, a middle, and a conclusion. The salesperson has *anticipated* questions and is prepared to answer them. The salesperson has practiced using his supportive aids and knows how to fit them into the discussion flow. The salesperson is ready to deliver the presentation from the client's position. When I said that the salesperson must have a good story to tell, I was talking about a solution to a need, not general conversation or chit-chat.

Mammoth's Fred ("Facts and Figures") Farrow could present details in an enthusiastic manner. He is an outgoing and friendly man. Fred played football in college and, except for a collapsible knee, is always in good shape. Despite his large, impressive size, Fred never tried to overpower people; he is a true gentle giant. He is a walking encyclopedia. He knows the dates, results, statistics, and prevailing weather of every game in almost every sport that has been played over the last 20 years.

Fred always prepared for a sales contact. He would studiously "bone-up" on the latest scores and sports news–who was sidelined, which manager was about to be released, or who had been thrown out of a game. He felt that it was his duty to keep all of his clients up to date on the latest sports information. Fred had probably the most knowledgeable clients around when it came to sports statistics. Unfortunately, many of his clients were not too sure about what Fred sold. As did a colleague of his at Mammoth, Fred had enthusiastic non-users. Recently he left Mammoth and joined the staff of a well-known purveyor of beer as a public relations man. His waistline is going to pot, but he finds that beer and sports statistics seem to go hand in hand.

Practice and Timing Skills

<u>Activities</u>	<u>Results</u>
Practice using the script.	This will give the presenter confidence and prepare him for the unexpected.
Practice using the script and visual aids together.	This will help the presenter to feel comfortable in front of other people.
Write the script or notes in large, bold letters.	This will help the presenter to maintain eye contact.
Practice without the script or visuals; they may get lost.	This will reduce the chance of stark panic if they should get lost or out of order.
Go through the presentation under the same conditions as the presentation will be given.	This will give the presenter a comfortable feel for the working area.
Have one or two colleagues act as the client audience. Have them participate, use questions, and role-play the client.	This will give the presenter a real-world feel for the flow of the presentation.
Have a colleague time and critique the presentation.	This will prevent the presenter from running out of time before he gets to the good stuff.

Practice with, and time, yourself.	This will help the presenter to both visualize the flow and pace the presentation to a successful conclusion.
Practice using all of the materials involved; then do it again.	This will help the presenter to deliver the presentation in a professional, successful manner.
Practice showing one visual at a time. Do not read a visual while facing away from the audience.	This will reduce the chance of losing contact with the audience.
Practice using handouts, samples, or other material that is to be circulated. The audience will focus their attention on *anything that moves.*	This will help the presenter to maintain control and interest.
Practice clarifying the contents of the material.	This will reduce the chance that hidden barriers will develop.
Practice what you will do if something unusual happens. Colleagues can be of great help in this practice activity.	Anticipating the unexpected gives the presenter the cool to handle a difficult situation.

From a one-on-one; across-the-table presentation to a multi-media formal presentation to a group, there is great value to practice. This will be evident to the client and will open the door to commitment.

THE PHYSICAL DELIVERY

The physical delivery of a sales talk or presentation can enhance or impede the results achieved. I have noted that good communication is *two-way* communication. There is a natural progression to a good presentation that has two-way communication flowing freely. When the solution has been presented effectively–when all questions have been answered and all objections have been overcome–a commitment usually follows.

Ken ("Keep Going") Keenan does not subscribe to this approach. He had, I imagine, been told at one time or another to keep talking; if you are talking, you are in control. Ken's idea of negotiative selling is to spell out everything that he had learned at Mammoth to every client.

Time stood still, and once he was on a roll nothing could stop him. He would plow ahead even if the client interrupted. This was being in control, and it did not allow the client to ask any difficult questions that Ken may not have been able to answer.

Ken Keenan uses the ethereal, televangelistic approach.

Ken's delivery is interesting. His technique is a "keep talking at all cost" delivery. This approach called for getting from A to Z as soon as possible, while ignoring signals, questions, or any other protestations by the client. Ken has a sonorous, rather melodic voice that after a while created a feeling of euphoria in the client. Buyers said that they felt a sense of "floating in space" as Ken talked on, resulting in a temporary separation from reality. The buyer would thank Ken for an uplifting presentation. Nothing, of course, was achieved. Not only was Ken talking about Mammoth from the seller's side of the table, he allowed his performance to get in the way of any worthwhile communication.

How to Control Those Strange Appendages
—One's Hands and Feet

Nervousness or apprehension will make the presenter aware of his performance, which will immediately be transmitted to the audience. As a result, he will become even more nervous and uncomfortable. Nervousness will affect the voice, the hands, and the feet. The presentation will come apart. Positive nervous energy is something quite different. When the presenter has *planned, prepared,* and *practiced* his presentation, he will be able to *channel* his energy toward his message and his audience. In a selling situation, an unprepared presenter will suddenly become aware that he or she actually has hands and feet. The hands take on a character of their own.

I noted earlier that all excessive movement will attract the client's eyes and concentration. If the salesperson is sitting across from a client, this nervousness will create an increase in hand movement. *Pen* or *pencil tapping* is one result. The salesperson will tap out morse code signals on the client's desk. The client will become intrigued and start to observe and listen to the message being tapped out. The sales presentation will be all but forgotten. *Pen rolling* can become the center of attention, with the client counting the number of revolutions. *Hand wringing* has a negative impact upon the client. He gets the feeling that the salesperson is about to take him to the cleaners. Playing with *rings, ties,* or *materials* will tend to make the client either like or dislike the tie or comment on the ring.

When the salesperson is standing, nervousness will result in a variety of hand movements:

- *Hands buried in pockets*, often rattling keys and spare change.
- *Prop holding:* I once saw a man bury a non-tipped pointer into a 50-page pad of chart paper. This takes super-human strength or extreme nervousness. A buyer told me he once observed a salesman holding a product sample for the entire length of his presentation. The buyer's mind was concentrating on the sample: "When is he going to do something with that sample?"
- *Markers* immediately become something to subconsciously open and close and to smear on shirt or blouse.
- *A script or 4" x 6" idiot cards* are immediately dropped on the floor.

Nervousness is also transmitted to the legs and feet, even when sitting down. I watched a presentation once with the salesperson sitting across the desk from the buyer. As the salesman started to talk, he crossed his legs, and the top leg immediately went into a toe-tapping routine. It was fascinating to watch the client's face. He could only see the salesman's knee bobbing up and down, so he gradually raised himself out of his chair to get a better look.

In a standing presentation, the legs and feet can create a great degree of distraction.

The *thumpers* are always interesting. They stand behind a podium with a foot on the lower shelf, which is usually about four inches off the floor. Nervousness is transmitted to the foot, and they start a rhythmic thumping. I have known situations wherein the audience joined in by clapping in unison, much to the chagrin of the unsuspecting presenter.

The *prowlers* are intriguing. They patrol backwards and forwards across the stage as they monotonously deliver their speech. Their hands go into prescribed positions:

- The Napoleon position: One hand thrust inside the jacket.
- The lawyer position: Hands grasping the jacket lapels.
- The "anyone for tennis" position: One hand inserted into the side pocket, with the thumb showing.

- The Ed Sullivan position: One arm held across the body to prop up the other forearm, while the hand covers the mouth.
- The casual position: Both hands held behind the back as the presenter patrols the stage, eyes fixed steadily ahead.
- The pockets position: This one is the worst. Both hands buried in one's pockets looks uncomfortable (which it is) and sloppy.

My favorite is the white-knuckle presenter. This person grasps each side of the podium and hangs on for dear life, his head buried in the script. Problems arise when he has to turn a page. The fact is, no one wants to become embarrassed or look like a fool when talking to an individual or group of people. A presenter who is unsure of himself can become overly sensitive to how he comes across. He forgets that the audience is not there to look at him; they want solutions. All of these problems can be overcome by converting nervousness into *productive energy* that is geared toward the presentation purpose. With good planning, preparation, and practice, the salesperson can guide the audience's attention toward the message and away from himself or herself.

Eye Contact

I noted in the first chapter of this book that the eyes must reflect what the mouth is saying. When the salesperson *believes* in what he is saying–when he projects that belief through his eyes–the client will respond. Conversely, when he is just talking and the client is looking into a blank pair of eyes, the client will probably think, "This person doesn't believe in what he is saying. How can he expect me to believe it?"

During my buyer surveys, I heard many complaints about eye contact:

- "He had a shifty-eyed, embarrassed look."
- "Couldn't look me in the eye. He stared at his notes the whole time."
- "She tried to stare me down. 1 will not play the first-one-to-blink-is-an-idiot game."
- "His eyes did not project his feelings; all I heard was words."

Sincerity, honesty, and enthusiasm will show in the eyes.

We have all had to sit through canned presentations. The presenter reads from a prepared script that was probably handed to him ten minutes earlier. There is no warmth, no feeling, no eye contact–just words. When I have to sit through one of these talks, I try to arrange a "watch committee" with another observer. We agree to make sure that neither of us falls off our chair.

Watch politicians, evangelists, or program hosts on television. Look into their eyes as you listen to their words. You will quickly recognize whether or not they believe what they are saying.

Voice, Speech, and Diction

We all have a natural voice range. When a salesperson pushes his voice into an unnatural range, it becomes distracting. Some salespeople try to deepen their voice range when they are making a presentation. They lose their normal pitch range and use an artificial basso monotone. The voice should be clearly projected *within* the presenter's range to avoid shouting. Professional actors practice using their voice to achieve shades of emphasis and range.

We are *not* actors. We should practice using this wonderful instrument as they do. Mumbling will quickly turn off the listener. Monotonous delivery will make the voice flat and uninteresting.

One of the best ways to develop the voice within its normal range is to read out loud. The presentation becomes much more effective when the presenter uses the full range of his voice. Emphasizing key points, using dramatic pauses, and end-of-sentence highlighting will give the presentation meaning. Underscoring impact points in a script will help. Try reading the newspaper out loud as if you are presenting it to an audience. Use punctuation marks as pause points. I recommend that salespeople join dramatic societies, debating teams, toastmasters, or any other organization that will give them a chance to practice using their voice.

The presenter's speech should be clear and concise. We noted that the salesperson's responsibility is to make the presentation interesting, without letting the performance get in the way of the message. I must say it one more time: There is no substitute for practice! Practice will help the salesperson to deliver difficult words without getting tongue-tied. If a word cannot be clearly pronounced, change it. Practice using video and/or audio tapes whenever possible.

Diction and enunciation are particularly important when technical data or other detailed information is being delivered. The choice of words, verbal style, and vocabulary that we use have a major impact upon our message. "Keep Going" Keenan fell in love with his own voice. Talking was more important than what he was saying. When we can consistently deliver a message that is clear, concise, easy to follow, and interesting to the other party, we get great personal satisfaction and positive results from the listener.

PRESENTING THE SOLUTION CHECKLIST

- The only thing that we have to sell is *client* benefits. Everything else is supportive.

- A benefit is the *tangible result* that the client receives from a product or service.

- Action verbs (trigger words) tell the client that it is a benefit:

–Increase	–Decrease	–Improve
–Expand	–Delete	–Save
–Define	–Eliminate	–Reduce

- Benefits can be used in statement or question form.

- Develop "Selling Blueprints" ahead of time. Each feature or detail provides its own benefits.

- Benefits can appeal to emotion.

- Benefits can appeal to logic.

- There are short- and long-term benefits.

- There are benefits that appeal to the client's own customers.

- Build and use a Company Attributes File.

- Use Comparative Analysis–how does your product or service compare with another? Use Strengths to Lesser Values.

- Clients make comparisons. Develop a comparative balance sheet.
- In the physical presentation, there is no substitute for practice.
- Confidence is contagious; so is apprehension.
- Practice and time the presentation.
- Control the hands and feet.
- Project nervous energy toward the message.
- Avoid playing with props. The client's eyes are drawn to movement, especially excessive movement.
- Don't prowl or wander around during the presentation.
- Maintain eye contact.
- Develop the voice within its normal range.
- Avoid mumbling or dull, monotonous delivery.
- The seller must believe in his solution if the buyer is to accept it.
- The listener is there to learn something, not to evaluate our performance.

Chapter 6

Turn Questions, Complaints, and Objections into Opportunities

Argument: A discussion which has two sides and no end.
—Leonard Neubauer

- I will anticipate questions and objections and prepare my response.
- I will handle the emotion that accompanies objections and use logic to resolve the problem.
- I will recognize that an objection can be turned into an opportunity.
- I will not become defensive or allow a problem to cause confrontation.

We all face questions, complaints, and objections:

- "I really don't understand this lengthy proposal. What does it all mean?"
- "This new system looks much more complicated than my present method."
- "I am afraid that this is a tough decision involving a major capital outlay. I must think about it for a while."
- "It must be made of gold."
- "I tried your service years ago and had a lot of problems. Probably nothing has changed today."

Questions, concerns, and objections can come up at any time during a sales contact. They must be handled honestly, straightforwardly, and effectively when they do arise, or a hidden objection will take root and a barrier to a successful sale will be created.

"Who needs bad news? Get into something positive as soon as possible." This is the opinion of Dan ("Dodge the Bullet") Dobson. Dan is a creative, selective listener. He hears words, but listens to what he really wants to hear. He uses a technique called "bridging into positives." When a client raises a tough question or objection Dan adopts an attitude of "I didn't hear that" and, with a smile, he bridges into something more palatable:

Dan: Mr. Wilson, our brass fittings have a wear ratio of 16.6% over a five-year span.

Mr. W.: What does that mean?

Dan (bridging): In addition, the brushed, polished appearance of these fittings enhances the beauty of the furniture.

Mr. W.: Tell me about this wear-ratio thing; how long will they last? You are not exactly giving them away.

Dan (bridging): Quality! Mr. Wilson. We have the reputation of being the Cadillac of the industry.

Mr. W.: Is that so?

Dan: Furthermore, independent tests have proved that Mammoth fittings outlast all other fittings manufacturers' products by 24.67%.

Mr. W.: Leave me a brochure. We will call you if we need you.

In this scenario, Dan did not answer the client's questions and concerns. He created a hidden objection. He lost the client's attention, his own credibility, and, very likely, any future business. The use of percentages (16.6% and 24.67%) mean very little to the client unless they can be converted into bottom-line revenue or figures.

Compare this with Tony ("True Blue") Thomasino's approach. Tony realizes that he must be prepared to answer questions and objections before he can get a commitment. He also knows that statements must be supported with testimonials and proof that stand up to the client's scrutiny. Tony is also aware that client benefits sell and that his product features are the logical source for benefits:

Tony: Mr. Wilson, you can provide your customers with brass fittings that will match the life of your quality product, and add to its appearance and salability with this attractive brush-polished design.

Mr. W.: I agree that they look nice; however, matching the life of our product sounds like an exaggeration to me.

Tony: I can understand your skepticism. Some statements do appear to be overstated. Let me show you this report based on a survey of a number of our established customers who have extensively used our fittings over the last ten years. Their individual comments are noted after each alphabetically listed customer.

Mr. W.: Interesting! These results would appear to support your life-expectancy claims for your fittings.

Tony has cleared up a concern, maintained the client's interest, and can now proceed with his sales story. By summarizing specific points during the sales negotiation–and supporting them with results achieved, data, testimonials, and proof (preferably from independent sources)–the salesperson keeps the client's thinking on track, reduces the chance of creating hidden objections, and helps him make a number of small decisions leading to commitment.

ANTICIPATING QUESTIONS AND OBJECTIONS

Professional salespeople believe that we should not dwell on negatives but concentrate on positive factors. I can't disagree with that. If we accept the fact that our clients are looking for help, for answers to their concerns, then *anticipating* questions and objections and preparing a *solution* ahead of time is a positive approach. We can turn objections into sales opportunities when we handle them correctly. When an objection catches us off guard, we can become defensive and lose the chance of solving a client problem.

TURNING OBJECTIONS INTO OPPORTUNITIES

Let's look more closely at the objections noted at the beginning of this chapter:

- "I really don't understand this lengthy proposal. What does it all mean?"

The client is defensive because he doesn't want to appear stupid. The salesperson must take the client through the proposal to clarify each point. The check question can be real valuable: "Mr. Jones, there is a lot of detail here. Is there a specific area that you would like reviewed?" If there is a portion that is isolated by the client, the salesperson can go through it again. If the client states that there is more than one portion that is complicated, the salesperson can cover each section and *qualify* it with check questions before moving on: "Mr. Jones, I probably moved through these points very quickly. This first part of the proposal covers . . ." Afterwards, verify: "Have I covered that to your satisfaction?"

- "This system looks much more complicated than my present method."

The client is comfortable with his present system. People resist change unless they can fully understand the new method and the *additional benefits* that they will receive when they make the change. For instance, you can reassure the client by stating: "Mr. Brown, you will find that your people will be happy with the new method. Our concentrated training program will make sure that they are fully conversant with the numbers. You will be able to reduce the number of man-hours that are required to meet your deadlines; eliminate the fatigue factor; reduce downtime and expensive service work; and increase your productivity in the bargain."

- "I am afraid that this is a tough decision involving major capital outlay. I must think about it for a while."

The client is nervous and apprehensive about making a major decision. The salesperson must search out the cause of the apprehension and use testimonials and proof to assure the client that he is making a sound decision, then support with benefits: "Mr. Harris, you can be assured that this unit will produce the higher productivity that you seek, with less downtime and virtually no maintenance required. The unit will pay for itself within two years, and then go on and save you additional money. Look at these industry statistics and other customer reports . . ."

- "It must be made of gold."

We looked earlier at the price objection. The client is saying, "What am I getting for my money?" The salesperson can introduce additional short- and long-term benefits that will justify the price asked. The company attribute file is valuable here: "Ms. Sherman, certainly cost is always a concern. I have prepared a list of *additional* benefits that will more than justify the cost of this program. As you can see . . ."

- "I tried your service years ago and had a lot of problems. Probably nothing has changed today."

The salesperson faces a credibility loss. He will have to show the client the improvements and advancements that exist in today's service and then support with testimonials and proof: "Mr. Rouch, as you may remember, the industry was going through some rapid changes at that time. Computerization was blossoming, creating constant service adjustments. Every one of us in the business ran into technical difficulties. We did learn a lot during that tough period, and we have applied what we learned to today's system. You will see here the built-in corrective factors in our new service that will offset any chance that this will happen again. Here is an up-to-date list of testimonials with the results that our clients have achieved without a single glitch."

Salespeople will face the same objections again and again in one form or another. In each of these examples, the salesperson can *anticipate* the questions or objections and work on a solution during the planning stage. An objections/solutions anticipation checklist will help. When we have at our fingertips the *basic* solution to many of the repetitive objections that we face, we can, with some adjustments, turn the objection into an opportunity. The client will recognize that here is someone who is big enough to face difficult questions and interested enough to develop an answer to the problem.

Below is an example of an objection that I have faced many times; the basic solution is also included. I will not be caught off guard again on this one:

Question/Concern/Objection	Logical Basic Solution
"Greening, I can't pull my people from the field for a three-day workshop."	"There never is a right time, I know; they have pretty big territories. Mr. Smith, if your salespeople could cover their territories *more effectively,* *avoid* back-tracking and *excessive* driving time, and make *more rewarding* sales calls, would you agree that the training time was well-spent?"

Try some of your own. What tough questions and objections do you face more than once? How would you handle them? What solution would you use?

Question/Concern/Objection	Logical Basic Solution
1.	1.
2.	2.

3.   3.

4.   4.

EMOTION AND ITS IMPACT
ON TWO-WAY COMMUNICATION

Positive emotion generates ideas and valuable input. One idea
triggers another. Creative juices flow and everyone is caught up in
the solution development project. I conduct peer-group workshops
with my clients. We have Problem Analysis/Solution Development
sessions in which we isolate major problem areas and then the
group establishes a solution(s). We start with the best possible solution, assuming we are provided with everything that we want, and
then expand the alternative solutions. It is rewarding to see positive
emotion and enthusiasm grow, while negative emotion, personal
hang-ups, and defensiveness recede. Now everyone is working together on the solution. Positive emotion is contagious!

Negative emotion will feed upon itself and grow if the cause is
not dealt with. When a client has a problem or a concern or raises an
objection, his emotion will overrule his logic. If the problem is not
cleared up, his negative emotion will increase. The salesperson's
first responsibility then is to reduce the client's emotion so that a
logical solution can be presented. When the salesperson addresses
the problem and *assures* the client that he or she is genuinely interested in resolving it, the client's negative emotion will subside and
logic takes over. Despite the emotional reaction, the client is looking for answers. It is difficult to stay on an emotional binge when
the other person is a sincere listener and shows interest and concern.

Consider the reaction of the client to these two different responses to his problem. In the first one, his negative emotions climb; in the second example, he is ready to accept a logical answer.

Client: What kind of a screwed-up outfit are you? In the last two shipments that your company sent us, we got incorrect part numbers, over 30% backorders, lousy packaging, and we received the damned invoice before the shipment arrived.

Salesperson: That really isn't my fault. I followed up on the order to make sure that it was shipped on time. I suspect what happened is that we are operating in our peak season and, as you probably know, the plant closed for two weeks last month for staff vacations. We are just getting back into full swing.

Client: I don't give a #*!§ whose fault it is. Our customers are unhappy, not to mention my salespeople. We don't have the luxury of taking two weeks' vacation together. I think that your company is fat and happy and is taking us for granted. It's time for us to take a serious look at your competitor.

The above client's emotions are climbing, and the salesperson has a real problem. In the following example, the salesperson shows the client he understands that a problem exists, assures the client that it will be handled speedily, and then sets in motion activities to resolve the problem.

Client: What kind of a screwed-up outfit are you? In the last two shipments that your company sent us, we got incorrect part numbers, over 30% backorders, lousy packaging, and we received the damned invoice before the shipment arrived.

Salesperson: I can understand your frustration. You have your customers to protect, and it is our job to support you in your marketing efforts. You are a fine account for us, and we value your business. I will do everything that I can to correct the problems we may have caused you, and I will make sure that it doesn't happen again.

Client: I don't want platitudes! I need some action *now!*

Salesperson: First, let me get the details of the incorrect part numbers and back-ordered parts. Then I will call the plant and get corrective action started right away. If I can use your spare office, I will stay here until I have this situation cleared up.

There are times when this approach is not right. When the client makes unreasonable demands or tries to put one over on the salesperson (or uses unethical practices), the salesperson should stand firm and use good judgment, based upon his own company policies. When the objection or problem is real, the salesperson can build personal and company prestige and satisfy a valued customer by being a concerned listener, assuring the customer that the problem will be handled, reducing emotion, and then working on a solution.

EFFECTIVELY HANDLING QUESTIONS AND OBJECTIONS CHECKLIST

- Handle each question or objection honestly, straightforwardly, and promptly.
- Anticipate questions and objections before they arise.
- Prepare basic solutions to questions or objections that come up often.
- Turn objections into opportunities.
- Use an objections/solutions anticipation checklist.
- Use testimonials and proof whenever doubt exists in the client's mind.
- Use additional benefits whenever possible to support your solution.
- Positive emotion is contagious.
- Reduce negative emotion before resolving the problem.
- Don't allow negative emotion to fester. Get the problem handled quickly.
- Always use good judgment, based upon company policies, when handling an objection.
- Don't make illogical promises that can come back to haunt you.
- Keep your emotions under control.
- Build your prestige, and the prestige of your company, by being an effective problem solver.

Chapter 7

How to Get Commitment

Confidence: That which compels you to do the thing that you think you cannot do.

–Anon.

- I will recognize the client's defined position.

- I will keep a list of requests for commitment.

- I will use the three-step close.

- I will have an alternative close available.

- I will keep quiet after I ask for an order.

Every skill examined thus far leads to one thing: getting commitment. Whether it is an order from a client, a commitment from a colleague, or a decision to move along a project, the presenter must persuade the listener to take action. From the salesperson's standpoint, the recommendations that have been made have to be converted into a negotiated close through a client agreement.

THE CLIENT'S DEFINED POSITION

The client has:

- A need for a solution to a problem that will improve his position.
- To be able to understand the short- and long-term benefits that he is offered.

- To see the benefits working for him and the results that they produce.
- To clearly see how the recommended solution works.
- To be supported and guided in the decision-making process.

If our recommendation follows the steps that have been covered in this book, the client is now at the fence-straddling stage: should I or shouldn't I buy? *How* the salesperson asks for the commitment has a significant bearing upon the outcome of the negotiation. I should also add *if* the salesperson asks for the order.

Freddy ("Last Furlong") Fotheringale is a likable person. He has a nice wife, nice kids, and a reasonably friendly dog. Freddy's house is nice. The yard is especially nice, with scattered, unobtrusive weeds. He has a nice sales manager (in Freddy's eyes) and, perish the thought, nice paperwork. He has a nice attitude: the cup is always half full. His clients and prospects like him; that is, up to the last furlong of his presentation. Freddy came by his nickname because of his habit of breaking down at the last furlong. He had searched out the client's needs, prepared his solution, built an excellent communications climate, presented benefits supported by features and details, and answered all questions and objections. But he could not ask for the order!

Freddy would wait for the client to *sell himself.* He would look at the client with a friendly smile on his face and an air of expectancy. (Come to think of it, Freddy's dog "Old Rorer" had the same expression at mealtimes.) There would be an awkward silence. Finally, the client would say those immortal words: "Don't call us. We will call you." Freddy gave no thought or planning to his close. He assumed that if he handled all of the other presentation skills, the client would sell himself. Sales presentations do not automatically come to a successful conclusion.

If Freddy had *confirmed the need,* summarized those benefits that had *been accepted* by the client, and then asked for the order, he would be far more successful. He could have said: "As we agreed then, Mr. Purchase, to help you to achieve your goals of penetrating those new market segments that you have targeted with a broader line of quality products, we will support you in a team blitz program and provide our line of high-quality, brush-polished fittings for your added product line. "With your approval, I will review your requirements based on the needs analysis and write an initial order. Would you want delivery in June or July?" In using this approach, Freddy would have built a positive platform leading to commitment. He would have given the client sound reasons to buy the Mammoth line. The client's thoughts are on the benefits that he expects to receive, not on the negatives of change.

There is really nothing difficult or complicated about asking for commitment if the salesperson *believes* in what he is selling. We all dislike rejection. This will happen, however, if the seller tries to sell a product rather than what it will do. If the client can see no value, he will reject the offer. A request for an order will either produce a *commitment* or it will uncover *resistance* or a *hidden objection* that must be cleared up. Confidence must be projected to the buyer. He wants to see and feel that the seller *knows* that his recommendation will get the results desired.

Apprehension comes from being insecure in the request for acceptance. Many good presentations fail to produce results because the salesperson hasn't given the closing of the sale the thought, planning, and effort that this all-important step requires. Remember these old chestnuts:

- "What do you think Mr. Brown?" (I have no idea.)
- "You will really appreciate this." (Wanna bet.)
- "Let me leave this brochure with you." (Why not?)
- "You don't have to decide right now." (In that case, I won't.)
- "When shall I come back to see you?" (In about a year.)
- "I'm not really looking for an order. My job is to keep our clients updated on product developments." (Send me a brochure next time.)
- "I suppose you are not ready yet to make a decision?" (Now that I think of it, you're right.)

What an absolute waste of time and effort to end a sales contact this way. I keep a list of requests for commitment, and I review this list prior to each sales contact. Which one will be most appropriate in this situation? When I have one that fits, I simply *modify* it to the circumstances. Some requests to follow:

- "Please sign this agreement, and I will get it moving right away."
- "What purchase order number do you want me to use?"
- "Let me have your letter-of-intent before I leave, and I can start to write the program."
- "To avoid any delay, what target date should we begin this project?"
- "Let's get started on it right away."

You may not want to use these examples. However, I do suggest that you be prepared with your own approaches *ahead of time.* You will be surprised how comfortable you are asking for the order.

THE THREE-STEP CLOSE

There are three steps to building a commitment foundation. This three-step approach takes the client's thought process along a logical path to an order. In this way, we will be able to avoid a sloppy, disorganized request for commitment. The client will feel the confidence that we project. The three steps are:

1. Restate and confirm the client's objective: "Mr. Brown, as we discussed, your objective is to expand your share of market in each trading area. Is that correct?"

2. Summarize only those key benefits that have been accepted by the client: "With this in mind, you will be able to *increase* the call ratio of your salespeople; *expand* their territories without losing existing customer contact; *enlarge* your customer base within each trading area; and *increase* your sales and profits with this revised marketing program."

3. Ask for the order: "If you have no further questions, please sign this order, and we can start to lay out the phase 1 approach."

THE CLOSE PRACTICE EXERCISE

Try some closing techniques of your own. You will be able to build a file that works for you.

Exercise #1

1. Restate and confirm the client's objective.

2. Summarize the key benefits that have been accepted by the client.

3. Ask for the order.

Exercise #2 (Use for One of Those Upcoming Sales Calls)

1.

2.

3.

Exercise #3

1.

2.

3.

Exercise #4

1.

2.

3.

AN ALTERNATIVE CLOSE OR FALLBACK POSITION

Once again, the planning stage comes into play here. If the sales-person asks himself, "What would I do if the client turns down my offer? What will I do to keep the sales contact alive? If I can't sell six widgets, perhaps I can sell three and build from there." The seller must guard against falling back on the alternative choice too quickly. The original objective should always be uppermost in the seller's mind. With a fallback position in his briefcase, the salesperson can avoid the possibility of folding up when the original request is refused.

AFTER ASKING FOR THE ORDER, KEEP QUIET AND WAIT

Before leaving this important skill of closing, there is one other valuable point to remember: After asking for the order, keep quiet! Wait for the client to come back. The ball is now in his court. This is hard for some salespeople to do. The normal inclination is to add supporting statements: "Random surveys have shown . . ." It is easy for any seller to talk themselves into, and out of, an order. Give the client a chance to think. Let him take the lead in the closing process.

HOW TO GET COMMITMENT CHECKLIST

- The client has a defined position:

  1. He wants a solution to a need or problem that will improve his position.
  2. He wants to be able to understand the short- and long-term benefits that he is offered.
  3. He wants to see the benefits working for him, and the results that they produce.
  4. He wants to clearly see how the recommended solution works.
  5. He wants to be supported and guided in the decision-making process.

- We must *believe* in what we are selling and how we can help the client to benefit.
- Cultivate the *desire* to close. Project confidence in the closing request.

- *Confidence* comes from the knowledge that the recommendation is sound.

- *Apprehension* comes from being insecure in the request for commitment.

- Plan and prepare the closing request ahead of time.

- Develop a list of requests for commitment. Write them down.

- Watch for buying signals. These signals will occur when the buyer starts to visualize the product or service working for him.

- The three-step close:
  1. Restate the client's objective.
  2. Summarize key benefits.
  3. Ask for the order.

- Keep the request straightforward and easy to understand.

- Be firm in the request, but avoid high-pressure tactics.

- A request for commitment will either produce an order or uncover a hidden objection.

- Have an alternative close or fallback position ready if the initial request is turned down.

- After asking for the order, keep quiet and let the client speak first.

- Keep the project alive. Plan follow-up activities immediately.

Chapter 8

Post-Call Analysis and Follow-Up

- I will use a progress report to bridge from one contact to the next.

- I will evaluate the results of the call as soon as possible after the contact.

- I will document all important information and plan my follow-up activities immediately.

- I will use a follow-up status action plan.

Have you ever had any of these situations happen to you?

- You had to make out a full week's worth of call reports on a Saturday? (What did I talk to Betty Jones about last Monday? There was something that I was supposed to get for her . . .)

- **Client:** Whatever happened to the market survey you promised me six months ago?

- **Boss:** Where is your report on that call you made on Memory Lane Records? The owner just called me and said that you were going to get back to him yesterday.

- You had an appointment with Tom Wilson for 10 a.m. today, and it's now 1 p.m.?

- **Spouse:** Do you know what today is?

When a salesperson leaves a client's business after a sales contact, he has a limited amount of time to *retain* and *document* all of the important points discussed during the session. Unless that information is documented right after the contact, most of it will be lost before the next sales call is made. Relying on one's memory, especially if more than one sales contact is made per day, will cause the salesperson a lot of grief and lost business.

THE CALL REPORT AS A PROGRESS REPORT

A call report is, or should be, a *progress* report. A call report that is structured as follows has no real value:

Client	Date	Discussed	Next Call
Memory Lane Records	10/1/92	Record distribution with Bill Brown.	11/1/92

Perhaps it does let the boss know that the salesperson is not sitting in a pub. (Of course, he may check.)

With a progress report we can *bridge* from one call to the next, maintain continuity, and keep everyone involved in the picture. A progress report will help us to acquire a client, and to keep that client over an extended period of time. We can alert all departments and people to the situation and what support that *we* need from them.

Bridging from a previous call should be a statement that *updates* the client on the major elements that were discussed during the last contact and *picks up* with the activities to be reviewed during the current meeting: "Mr. Brown, at our last meeting on August 26th, we discussed your expansion into the truck tire market. You requested information on past opening sales action plans and how we worked with each dealer to set up the initial joint blitz program. I now have this information for you. Let me first show you . . . "

In most professional sales situations, an order is a *step* in building long-term, productive business relationships. To build a *client file*, the salesperson documents the results (or lack of them) of each contact. Then, if the client states, "In your letter of two years ago last March, you noted that we would have an exclusive franchise," the salesperson can pull the correct information out of the file.

When writing a call report, consider the following points:

- What do I need to know after the contact?
- What did I achieve?
- What didn't I achieve?
- Why wasn't it achieved?
- What help do I need?
- What is my next move?

POST-SALES CALL PROGRESS ANALYSIS

Many salespeople use a simple form that works for them. I use one that has really helped me to follow up on my sales contacts. I design and write marketing programs for my clients. There is usually a fair amount of input during the needs analysis sessions, and as a result, my progress file becomes full. Without it I would be lost. A copy of my analysis form follows at the end of this chapter.

FOLLOW-UP STATUS ACTION PLAN

Team selling projects can fall down when the required follow-up activities are allowed to collapse. The situation may be a multiple-location account that requires a number of salespeople to contact branches. The sales manager may even participate.

The project may require a number of departments to be involved, along with various people from other areas of the company. In a situation such as this, communication is essential. There is a place for verbal communication; however, the risk of misinterpretation and misunderstanding is always present. To keep the project rolling–and to make everyone aware of what has to be done and by whom–a follow-up status action plan can be of real value.

What are the benefits to salespeople if they use a sound post-call analysis and follow-up system? They can:

- Make sure that the two-way communication with the client is accurate and factual.

- Avoid missed or misunderstood detail.
- Eliminate the chance that the project will get bogged down.
- Use in-house resources that will add value to the process. (Perhaps the chief accountant should be on the next call.)
- Establish target dates that keep the program alive and on schedule.
- Build personal and company prestige.
- Take the project through to a successful conclusion.
- Close more deals and make more money.
- Enjoy the satisfaction that comes from a job well-done.

FOLLOW-UP STATUS ACTION PLAN

OBJECTIVE_____   DATE_____

PROJECT/TEAM STATUS_____

ACTIVITIES REQUIRED	INDIVIDUAL RESPONSIBILITY	TARGET DATE	PROGRESS STATUS
1.			
2.			
3.			
4.			

ADDITIONAL COMMENTS_____

POST-SALES CALL PROGRESS ANALYSIS

DATE OF SALES CALL _____   CLIENT/LOCATION _____

CALL OBJECTIVE _____

WHAT WAS ACHIEVED? _____   WHAT WAS NOT ACHIEVED? _____
_____   _____
_____   _____

WHY WAS IT NOT ACHIEVED? _____   WHAT HELP OR SUPPORT DO I NEED? _____
_____   _____
_____   _____

WHAT ACTION IS NOW NECESSARY? _____
_____
_____

ADDITIONAL COMMENTS/OBSERVATIONS _____
_____
_____

Chapter 9

A Selling Attitude

Experience: (That which) makes a person better or bitter.

–Samuel Levenson

- I will maintain a positive attitude.

- I will overcome my frustration when things go wrong.

- I will never stop learning, and will always look for a better method.

- I will always enjoy working with people–even the difficult ones.

- I will always be a professional salesperson.

One of the most important selling tools in any salesperson's tool bag is a positive attitude. We have a tough, demanding job that can be frustrating. It can also be satisfying and rewarding. We must be tenacious. It takes guts to get up off the floor when we have been knocked on our butts, to dust ourselves off, and then go back in through the side door: "As I was saying before I was rudely interrupted . . ." We enjoy helping people to achieve their goals. That's professional selling! When our client benefits, we benefit. I still remember the young salesman who took over a territory in Seattle. He battled tough odds, but never lost his positive attitude and his desire to help his clients and prospects.

During a recent buzz session with one of my groups of students, we tackled the subject of frustration: What creates it and how to overcome it. True to my belief in checklists, we set up two chart pads and went at it. The following list is the outcome. I keep this list in front of me and refer to it each morning before I make my first sales call.

HOW TO OVERCOME FRUSTRATION

- Avoid negative, "bucket dumping" sessions with other people. Accentuate the positive.
- Do not take business setbacks as personal setbacks. Critique the activity, not the person.
- Don't carry today's setbacks over to tomorrow. Work on the solution, not the frustration, in the morning.
- Don't fret over missed deliveries, backorders, or shortages. Look for better solutions or better ways to accomplish results.
- Completely ignore the company rumor mill. Wait until you see it in writing before you believe it.
- When that telephone rings, it's our livelihood calling.
- Reverse Murphy's Law: Whatever can go *right* will.
- Remember that colleagues and clients are human beings and prone to the same frustrations.
- Keep that sense of humor. Learn to laugh at yourself once in a while.
- Smile! Everyone has an attractive smile.
- Be an interested, concerned listener.
- Build a "relating habit" with colleagues and clients.
- The cup is always half full–never half empty.
- Enjoy your work. Feel good about yourself and your accomplishments.
- Always give 110%.
- Avoid procrastination! Quit complaining and get it done.

HOW TO BUILD AND MAINTAIN
A POSITIVE SELLING ATTITUDE

- A thorough knowledge of the products and services that we sell.
- A thorough knowledge of the client and his or her needs.

- A thorough knowledge of the competitors–their strengths and lesser values.
- Planning, preparing, and practicing for each sales contact.
- The effective use of questioning and listening skills to establish the client's objectives.
- Presenting those benefits that address the client's needs and supporting them with features, details, and testimonials.
- Anticipating questions and objections, and knowing how to handle them.
- Knowing how to ask for commitment and what to do if the request meets resistance.
- Maintaining a sincere belief in the strengths of our organization–its people, products, and services.
- Maintaining a sincere belief in ourselves, coupled with a desire to be of help to others.
- Tomorrow will be our most productive selling day–I know it!

As we grow in this great profession of ours, we will learn something new every day. There is always a better way to do everything if we look for it. I continuously learn new approaches and methods. When the day comes that I stop learning, I will hang up my briefcase. I know of no other profession that gives a person a chance to meet so many interesting people and work on so many interesting projects. Good Selling!

Call or write for information about in-house sales training workshops, writing, and guest speaking assignments.

Jack Greening
Productive Communications
P.O. Box 2497
1222 Linwood Avenue S.W.
North Canton, Ohio 44720
(216) 494–3293

Index

Accounting systems managers, 48
Action verbs
    presenting solutions, 58-59,81
    three-step close, 96
Anticipation
    of client requests, 19-21
    of questions and objections, 85
Attitude
    building and maintaining, 108-109
    communication, 32-33
    goals, 107-108
    overcoming frustration, 108
Attributes of companies' blueprints,
    67-68

Banks, 47
Benefits
    benefit/feature analysis practice,
      59-60
    checklist, 81
    in company attribute blueprint,
      67-68
    defined, 58-59
    in selling blueprint, 60-66
Blueprints
    company attribute, 67-68
    selling, 60-66,69
Brochures in sales call, 21-22
Business climate and
      communication
    building, 32-33
    checklist, 36-38
    client feelings, 31-32
    goals, 29-31
    practice exercise, 38-39
    professional image, 33-36

Call reports
    action plan, 103-106
    analysis, 103
    as progress reports, 102-103
Charts in sales call, 21-22. *See also*
    Planning a sales call
Checklists
    building and maintaining positive
      attitude, 108-109
    client needs analysis, 43-44
    communication, 36-38
    follow-up status action plan,
      103-104
    getting commitment, 99-100
    handling questions and objections,
      91
    overcoming frustration, 108
    pre-call preparation, 26-28
    presenting solutions, 81-82
    questions in uncovering client
      needs, 48
    sales call planning
      activities, 16
      first-time fact-finding, 11-12
Clients
    anticipating requests, 19-21
    commitment, 93-100
    communication, 31-32
    crossed viewpoints, 5
    needs and presentation
      of solutions
      benefits, 58-60
      checklist, 81-82
      company attribute blueprint,
        67-68
      comparative analysis, 69-72
      goals, 57-58
      internal selling, 67